1 MONTH OF
FREE
READING

at
www.ForgottenBooks.com

By purchasing this book you are eligible for one month membership to ForgottenBooks.com, giving you unlimited access to our entire collection of over 1,000,000 titles via our web site and mobile apps.

To claim your free month visit:
www.forgottenbooks.com/free1012595

ISBN 978-0-331-08566-2
PIBN 11012595

For support please visit www.forgottenbooks.com

A SHORT

ACCOUNT

OF THE

MALIGNANT FEVER,

LATELY PREVALENT IN

PHILADELPHIA:

WITH A STATEMENT OF THE

PROCEEDINGS

THAT TOOK PLACE ON THE SUBJECT, IN DIFFERENT
PARTS OF THE

UNITED STATES.

———

TO WHICH ARE ADDED,

ACCOUNTS

OF THE

Plague in London and Marseilles;

AND A LIST OF THE DEAD,

From Auguſt 1, to the middle of December, 1793.

BY MATHEW CAREY.

FOURTH EDITION, IMPROVED.

To the American Philofophical Society.

GENTLEMEN,

WITH due deference, I prefume to dedicate to you the following pages, in which I have endeavoured to give as faithful an account as poffible, of the dreadful calamity we have juft experienced.

I am, gentlemen,

With efteem,

Your obedt. humble fervant,

MATHEW CAREY.

NUMBER XLVII.

Diſtrict of Pennſylvania, to wit—

(L. S.) **B**E it remembered, that on the thirteenth day of November, in the eighteenth year of the independence of the united ſtates of America, Mathew Carey, of the ſaid diſtrict, hath depoſited in this office, the title of a book, the right whereof he claims as author, in the words following, to wit :

" *A ſhort account of the malignant fever lately* " *prevalent in Philadelphia, with a ſtatement of the* " *proceedings that took place on the ſubject in different* " *parts of the united ſtates. By Mathew Carey.*" In conformity to the act of the congreſs of the united ſtates, intituled, " *An act for the encouragement of* " *learning; by ſecuring the copies of maps, charts,* " *and books, to the authors and proprietors of ſuch* " *copies, during the times therein mentioned.*"

S A M U E L   C A L D W E L L, *Clerk of* the diſtrict of Pennſylvania.

PREFACE

FIRST EDITION.

Philadelphia, Nov. 13, 1793.

THE favourable reception given to the imperfect account of the fever which I lately publifhed, and the particular defire of fome of my friends, have induced me to undertake a more fatisfactory hiftory of it, in order to collect together, while facts are recent, as many of the moft interefting occurrences as I could, for the information of the public.

I have not attempted any embellifhment or ornament of ftile ; but have merely aimed at telling plain facts in plain language. I have taken every precaution to arrive at the truth ; aud hope the errors in the account, will not be found numerous.

For the defultory plan of fome part of the pamphlet, I have to offer the following apology ; many of the circumftances and reflections towards the conclufion, which would have come with more propriety in the beginning, did not occur, until fome of the firft half-fheets were not only written, but printed. I had no choice, therefore, but either to omit them, or place them fomewhat out of order. I preferred the latter.

Moft of the facts mentioned have fallen under my own obfervation. Thofe of a different defcription, I have been affiduous to collect from every perfon of credibility, poffeffed of information.

Defirous of having this account correct and complete, I have printed off but a fmall number of copies of the prefent edition : and fhall efteem myfelf moft particularly obliged to any perfon who will be fo kind to point out errors, to be corrected in, or fuggeſt facts, to be added to, a new edition, which I propoſe to put to preſs very ſoon, and which will, I hope, be found more ample than the preſent one.

PREFACE to the SECOND EDITION.

November 23, 1793.

WHEN I publiſhed the firſt edition of this pamphlet, it was my intention to have greatly enlarged it for a ſecond one, and to have new-modelled it, ſo as to preſerve a connexion between its ſeveral parts, in which it is extremely deficient. But its ſpeedy ſale, and the demand for more copies, render it impoſſible for me to do more, at preſent, than make ſuch corrections as the kindneſs of a few friends has led them to point out.

In giving an account of the proceedings that took place on the ſubject of the diſorder, throughout the union, I have ſuppreſſed many a harſh comment, which was forcing itſelf on me; from the reflexion, that in ſimilar circumſtances, we might perhaps have been equally ſevere. And to perpetuate animoſities, is performing a very unfriendly office. They are eaſily generated; but their extinction is a work of time and difficulty. Let us, therefore, (eſpecially when we " hold the mirror up to nature" at home,) not only forgive, but even forget, if poſſible, all the unpleaſant treatment our citizens have experinced.

I have heard more than one perſon object to the account of the ſhocking circumſtances that occurred in Philadelphia, as pourtraying the manners of the people in an unfavourable light. If that be the caſe, the fault is not mine. I am conſcious I have not exaggerated the matter. But I do not conceive it can have that effect; for it would be as unjuſt and injudicious to draw the character of Philadelphia from the proceedings of a period of horror and affright, when all the " mild charities of ſocial life" were ſuppreſſed by regard for felf, as to ftamp eternal infamy on a nation, for the atrocities perpetrated in times of civil broils, when all the " angry paffions" are roufed into dreadful and ferocious activity.

PREFACE to the THIRD EDITION.

November 30, 1793.

THIS pamphlet comes before the public a third time, and, in, fome meafure, in a new form. I have reduced it to as methodical a ftate, as, in my power, but not as much fo as I could wifh, nor, I fear, as the reader may expect. To one merit only do I lay claim in the compilation ; that is, of having meant well. If, on a fair perufal, the candid allow me that, I am fatis-fied to' have the execution cenfured with all the feve-rity of which criticifm is capable. However, I beg leave to inform the reader, that this day ends one month, fince the writing of the pamphlet commenced. I know that the fhortnefs of the time employed, is no juftifi-cation of a bad performance ; but it may fomewhat extenuate the defects of a middling one.

I have found feveral objections made to parts of it. Moft of them I have removed. Some few, refting on the fentiments of individuals, directly contrary to my own judgment, I have paffed over. For, until my reafon is convinced, I cannot change my opinion for that of any perfon whatever.

To thofe gentlemen who have been fo kind to fur-nifh me with facts to enlarge and improve the work, I profefs myfelf under great obligations. I requeft them to continue their kindnefs ; as, if public favour fhould give this trifle a fourth edition, I fhall add all that may be communicated in the interim; otherwife I fhall probably publifh feparately what may be worthy of the public eye.

PREFACE TO THE FOURTH EDITION.

Jan. 16, 1794.

THE uncommon degree of favour which this pamphlet has experienced, has impreſſed me with lively ſentiments of gratitude. As the only proper return in my power, I have, in each ſucceſſive edition, uſed every endeavour to improve it.

In the number of victims to the late calamity, there were many ſtrangers,—among whom were probably ſome, by whoſe death, eſtates have fallen to heirs at a diſtance. It being, therefore, of great importance to extend and improve the liſt of the dead, and to remedy the extreme inaccuracy of the ſextons' returns, I employed ſuitable perſons to go thro' the city and liberties, and make enquiry at every houſe, without exception, for the names and occupations of the dead. The diſobliging temper of ſome, and the fears of others, that an improper uſe would be made of the information they could have given, have, in various inſtances, defeated my purpoſe. Imperfect as the liſt ſtill remains, I hope it will be found uſeful in removing anxious doubts, and conveying to perſons in different countries, the melancholy information of the deceaſe of relatives, which, but for ſuch a channel of communication, would, in many caſes, be difficult, if not impoſſible to acquire for years to come.

To the preſent edition, I have added a ſhort account of the plague at London, and at Marſeilles. On a compariſon, the reader will be ſtruck with aſtoniſhment, at the extraordinary ſimilarity between many of the leading and moſt important circumſtances that occurred in thoſe two places, and the events of September and October, 1793, in Philadelphia.

———

Chap. I. State of Philadelphia previous to the appearance of the malignant fever—with a few observations on some of the probable consequences of that calamity.

BEFORE I enter on the consideration of this disorder, it may not be improper to offer a few introductory remarks on the situation of Philadelphia previous to its commencement, which will reflect light on some of the circumstances mentioned in the course of the narrative.

The manufactures, trade, and commerce of this city, had, for a considerable time, been improving and extending with great rapidity. From the period of the adoption of the federal government, at which time America was at the lowest ebb of distress, her situation had progressively become more and more prosperous. Confidence, formerly banished, was universally restored. Property of every kind, rose to, and in some instances beyond, its real value; and a few revolving years exhibited the interesting spectacle of a young country, with a new form of government, emerging from a state which approached very near to anarchy, and acquiring all the stability and nerve of the best-toned and oldest nations.

In this prosperity, which revived the almost-extinguished hopes of four millions of people, Philadelphia participated in an eminent degree. Numbers of new houses, in almost every street, built in a very neat, elegant stile, adorned, at the same time that they greatly enlarged, the city. Its population was extending fast. House-rent had risen to an extravagant height; it was in many cases double, and in some

B

treble what it had been a year or two before; and, as is generally the cafe, when a city is advancing in profperity, it far exceeded the real increafe of trade. The number of applicants for houfes, exceeding the number of houfes to be let, one bid over another; and affairs were in fuch a fituation, that many people, though they had a tolerable run of bufinefs, could hardly do more than clear their rents, and were, literally, toiling for their landlords alone*. Luxury, the ufual, and perhaps inevitable concomitant of prof-perity, was gaining ground in a manner very alarm-ing to thofe who confidered how far the virtue, the liberty, and the happinefs of a nation depend on its temperance and fober manners.—Many of our citi-zens had been, for fome time, in the imprudent habit of regulating their expenfes by profpects formed in fanguine hours, when every probability was caught at as a certainty, not by their actual profits, or in-come. The number of coaches, coachees, chairs, &c. lately fet up by men in the middle rank of life, is hardly credible. Not to enter into a minute detail, let it fuffice to remark, that extravagance, in various forms, was gradually eradicating the plain and whole-fome habits of the city. And although it were pre-fumption to attempt to fcan the decrees of heaven, yet few, I believe, will pretend to deny, that fome-thing was wanting to humble the pride of a city, which was running on in full career, to the goal of prodigality and diffipation.

However, from November 1792, to the end of laft June, the difficulties of Philadelphia were extreme. The eftablifhment of the bank of Pennfylvania, in embryo for the moft part of that time, had arrefted in the two other banks fuch a quantity of the circulat-ing fpecie, as embarraffed almoft every kind of bufi-nefs; to this was added the diftrefs arifing from the very numerous failures in England, which had

* The diftrefs arifing from this fource, was perhaps the only exception to the general obfervation of the flourifhing fitua-tion of Philadelphia.

extremely harraſſed ſeveral of our capital merchants. During this period, many men experienced as great difficulties as were ever known in this city*. But the commencement, in July, of the operations of the bank of Pennſylvania, conducted on the moſt generous and enlarged principles, placed buſineſs on its former favourable footing. Every man looked forward to this fall as likely to produce a vaſt extenſion of trade. But how fleeting are all human views! how uncertain all plans founded on earthly appearances! All theſe flattering proſpects vaniſhed " like the baſeleſs fabric of a viſion."

In July, arrived the unfortunate fugitives from Cape François. And on this occaſion, the liberality of Philadelphia was diſplayed in a moſt reſpectable point of light. Nearly 12,000 dollars were in a few days collected for their relief. Little, alas! did many of the contributors, then in eaſy circumſtances, imagine, that a few weeks would leave their wives and children dependent on public charity, as has ſince unfortunately happened. An awful inſtance of the rapid and warning viciſſitudes of affairs on this tranſitory ſtage.

About this time, this deſtroying ſcourge, the malignant fever, crept in among us, and nipped in the bud the faireſt bloſſoms that imagination could form. And oh! what a dreadful contraſt has ſince taken place! Many women, then in the lap of eaſe and contentment, are bereft of beloved huſbands, and left with numerous families of children to maintain, unqualified for the arduous taſk—many orphans are deſtitute of parents to foſter and protect them—many entire families are ſwept away, without leaving " a trace behind"—many of our firſt commercial houſes are totally diſſolved, by the death of the parties, and

---

* It is with great pleaſure, I embrace this opportunity of declaring, that the very liberal conduct of the bank of the united ſtates, at this trying ſeaſon, was the means of ſaving many a deſerving and induſtrious man from ruin. No ſimilar inſtitution was ever conducted on a more favourable, and at the ſame time, prudent plan, than this bank adopted at the time here mentioned.

their affairs are necessarily left in so deranged a state, that the losses and distresses which must take place, are beyond estimation. The protests of notes for a few weeks past, have exceeded all former examples; for a great proportion of the merchants and traders having left the city, and been totally unable, from the stagnation of business, and diversion of all their expected resources, to make any provision for payment, most of their notes have been protested, as they became due*.

For these prefatory observations, I hope I shall be pardoned. I now proceed to the melancholy subject I have undertaken. May I be enabled to do it justice; and lay before the reader a complete and correct account of the most awful visitation that ever occurred in America. At first view, it would appear that Philadelphia alone felt the scourge; but its effects have spread in almost every direction through a great portion of the union. Many parts of Jersey, Delaware, Maryland, Virginia, North and South Carolina, and Georgia, exclusive of the back settlements of Pennsylvania, drew their supplies, if not wholly, at least principally, from Philadelphia, which was of course the mart whither they sent their produce. Cut off from this quarter, their merchants have had to seek out other markets, which being unprepared for such an increased demand, their supplies have been imperfect; and, owing to the briskness of the sales, the prices have been, naturally enough, very considerably enhanced. Besides, they went to places in which their credit was not established—and had in most cases to advance cash. And many country dealers have had no opportunity of sending their produce to market, which has consequently remained unsold. Business, therefore, has languished in many parts of the union; and it is

* The bank of the united states, on the 15th of October, passed a resolve, empowering the cashier to renew all discounted notes, when the same drawers and indorsers were offered, and declaring that no notes should be protested, when the indorsers bound themselves in writing, to be accountable in the same manner as in cases of protest.

probable, that, confidering the matter merely in a commercial point of light, the fhock caufed by the fever, has been felt to the fouthern extremity of the united ftates.

C H A P. II.—*Symptoms—a flight fketch of the mode of treatment.*

" THE fymptoms which characterifed the firft ftage of the fever, were, in the greateft number of cafes, after a chilly fit of fome duration, a quick, tenfe pulfe—hot fkin—pain in the head, back, and limbs—flufhed countenance—inflamed eye—moift tongue—oppreffion and fenfe of forenefs at the ftomach, efpecially upon preffure—frequent fick qualms, and retchings to vomit, without difcharging any thing, except the contents laft taken into the ftomach—coftivenefs, &c. And when ftools were procured, the firft generally fhowed a defect of bile, or an obftruction to its entrance into the inteftines. But brifk purges generally altered this appearance.

" Thefe fymptoms generally continued with more or lefs violence from one to three, four, or even five days ; and then gradually abating, left the patient free from every complaint, except general debility. On the febrile fymptoms fuddenly fubfiding, they were immediately fuccecded by a yellow tinge in the opaque cornea, or whites of the eyes—an increafed oppreffion at the præcordia—a conftant puking of every thing taken into the ftomach, with much ftraining, accompanied with a hoarfe, hollow noife.

" If thefe fymptoms were not foon relieved, a vomiting of matter, refembling coffee grounds in colour and confiftence, commonly called the black vomit, fometimes accompanied with, or fucceeded by hæmorrhages from the nofe, fauces, gums, and other parts of the body—a yellowifh purple colour, and putrefcent appearance of the whole body, hiccup, agitations, deep and diftreffed fighing, comatofe delirium, and finally, death. When the difeafe proved fatal, it was generally between the fifth and eighth days.

" This was the most usual progress of this formidable disease, through its several stages. There were, however, very considerable variations in the symptoms, as well as in the duration of its different stages, according to the constitution and temperament of the patient, the state of the weather, the manner of treatment, &c.

" In some cases, signs of putrescency appeared at the beginning, or before the end of the third day. In these, the black vomiting, which was generally a mortal symptom, and universal yellowness, appeared early. In these cases, also, a low delirium, and great prostration of strength, were constant symptoms, and coma came on very speedily.

" In some, the symptoms inclined more to the nervous than the inflammatory type. In these, the jaundice colour of the eye and skin, and the black vomiting, were more rare. But in the majority of cases, particularly after the nights became sensibly cooler, all the symptoms indicated violent irritation and inflammatory diathesis. In these cases, the skin was always dry, and the remissions very obscure.

" The febrile symptoms, however, as has been already observed, either gave way on the third, fourth, or fifth day, and then the patient recovered; or they were soon after succeeded by a different, but much more dangerous train of symptoms, by debility, low pulse, cold skin, (which assumed a tawny colour, mixed with purple) black vomiting, hæmorrhages, hiccup, anxiety, restlessness, coma, &c. Many, who survived the eighth day, though apparently out of danger, died suddenly in consequence of an hæmor. rhage*."

This disorder having been new to nearly all our physicians, it is not surprising, although it has been exceedingly fatal, that there arose such a discordance of sentiment on the proper mode of treatment, and even with respect to its name. Dr. Rush has acknow.

---

* For this account of the symptoms of the disorder, I am indebted to the kindness of dr. Currie, from whose letter to dr. Sexter, it is extracted.

ledged, with a candour that does him honour, that in the commencement, he so far mistook the nature of the disorder, that in his early essays, having depended on gentle purges of salts to purify the bowels of his patients, they all died. He then tried the mode of treatment adopted in the West Indies, viz. bark, wine, laudanum, and the cold bath, and failed in three cases out of four. Afterwards he had recourse to strong purges of calomel and jalap, and to bleeding, which he found attended with singular success.

The honour of the first essay of mercury in this disorder, is by many ascribed to dr. Hodge and dr. Carson, who are said to have employed it a week before dr. Rush. On this point, I cannot pretend to decide. But whoever was the first to introduce it, one thing is certain, that its efficacy was great, and rescued many from death. I have known, however, some persons, who, I have every reason to believe, fell sacrifices to the great reputation this medicine acquired; for in several cases it was administered to persons of a previous lax habit, and brought on a speedy dissolution.

I am credibly informed that the demand for purges of calomel and jalap, was so great, that some of the apothecaries could not mix up every dose in detail; but mixed a large quantity of each, in the ordered proportions; and afterwards divided it into doses; by which means, it often happened that one patient had a much larger portion of calomel, and another of jalap, than was intended by the doctors. The fatal consequences of this may be easily conceived.

An intelligent citizen, who has highly distinguished himself by his attention to the sick, says, that he found the disorder generally come on with costiveness; and unless that was removed within the first twelve hours, he hardly knew any person to recover; on the contrary, he says, as few died, on whom the cathartics operated within that time.

The efficacy of bleeding, in all cases not attended with putridity, was great. The quantity of blood taken was in many cases astonishing. Dr. Griffits was bled seven times in five days, and appears to afcribe his recovery principally to that operation. Dr. Meafe, in five days, loft feventy-two ounces of blood, by which he was recovered when at the loweft ftage of the diforder. Many others were bled ftill more, and are now as well as ever they were.

Dr. Rufh and dr. Wiftar have fpoken very favourably of the falutary effects of cold air, and cool drinks, in this diforder. The latter fays, that he found more benefit from cold air, than from any other remedy. He lay delirious, and in fevere pain, between a window and door, the former of which was open. The wind fuddenly changed, and blew full upon him, cold and raw. Its effects were fo grateful, that he foon recovered from his delirium—his pain left him—in an hour he became perfectly reafonable—and his fever abated.

A refpectable citizen who had the fever himfelf, and likewife watched its effects on eleven of his family, who recovered from it, has informed me, that a removal of the fick from a clofe, warm room to one a few degrees cooler, which practice he employed feveral times daily, produced a moft extraordinary and favourable change in their appearance, in their pulfe, and in their fpirits.

CHAP. III.—*Firft alarm in Philadelphia. Flight of the citizens. Guardians of the poor borne down with labour.*

IT was fome time before the diforder attracted public notice. It had in the mean while fwept off many perfons. The firft death that was a fubject of general converfation, was that of Peter Afton, on the 19th of Auguft, after a few days illnefs. Mrs. Lemaigre's, on the day following, and Thomas Miller's, on the 25th, with thofe of fome others, after a fhort ficknefs, fpread an univerfal terror.

The removals from Philadelphia began about the 25th or 26th of this month: and fo great was the general terror, that, for fome weeks, carts, waggons, coachees, and chairs, were almoft conftantly tranfporting families and furniture to the country in every direction. Many people shut up their houses wholly; others left servants to take care of them. Business then became extremely dull. Mechanics and artists were unemployed; and the streets wore the appearance of gloom and melancholy.

The first official notice taken of the disorder, was on the 22d of August, on which day the mayor of Philadelphia, Matthew Clarkson, esq. wrote to the city commissioners, and after acquainting them with the state of the city, gave them the most peremptory orders, to have the streets properly cleansed and purified by the scavengers, and all the filth immediately hawled away. These orders were repeated on the 27th, and similar ones given to the clerks of the market.

. The 26th of the same month, the college of physicians had a meeting, at which they took into consideration the nature of the disorder, and the means of prevention and of cure. They published an address to the citizens, signed by the president and secretary, recommending to avoid all unnecessary intercourse with the infected; to place marks on the doors or windows where they were; to pay great attention to cleanliness and airing the rooms of the sick; to provide a large and airy hospital in the neighbourhood of the city for their reception; to put a stop to the tolling of the bells; to bury those who died of the disorder in carriages, and as privately as possible; to keep the streets and wharves clean; to avoid all fatigue of body and mind, and standing or sitting in the sun, or in the open air; to accommodate the dress to the weather, and to exceed rather in warm than in cool clothing; and to avoid intemperance; but to use fermented liquors, such as wine, beer and cider, with moderation. They likewise declared their opinion, that fires in the streets were very dangerous, if not ineffectual means of stopping the progress of the fever, and that they placed more dependance on the burning of gunpowder. The benefits of vinegar and camphor, they added, were confined chiefly to infected rooms; and they could not be too often

C

ufed on handkerchiefs, or in fmelling bottles, by perfons who attended the fick.

. In confequence of this addrefs, the bells were immediately ftopped from tolling. The expedience of
this measure was obvious ; as they had before been
conftantly ringing almoft the whole day, fo as to terrify thofe in health, and drive the fick, as far as the
influence of imagination could produce that effect,
to their graves. An idea had gone abroad, that the
burning of fires in the ftreets, would have a tendency
to purify the air, and arreft the progrefs of the difi-
order. The people had, therefore, almoft every night,
large fires lighted at the corners of the ftreets. The
29th, the mayor, conformably with the opinion of the
college of phyficians, publifhed a proclamation, for-
bidding this practice. As a fubftitute, many had recourfe to the firing of guns, which they imagined was
a certain preventative of the diforder. This was carried fo far, and attended with fuch danger, that it was
forbidden by an ordinance of the mayor.

The 29th, the governor of the ftate wrote a letter to
the mayor, ftrongly enforcing the neceffity of the moft
vigorous and decifive exertions " to prevent the extenfion of, and to deftroy, the evil." He defired that
the various directions given by the college of phyficians, fhould be carried into effect. The fame day, in
his addrefs to the legiflature, he acquainted them, that
a contagious diforder exifted in the city ; and that he
had taken every proper meafure to afcertain the origin, nature, and extent of it. He likewife affured them
that the health-officer and phyfician of the port,
would take every precaution to allay and remove
the public inquietude.

The number of the infected daily increafing, and the
exiftence of an order againft the admiffion of perfons
labouring under infectious difeafes into the alms-
houfe, precluding them from a refuge there*, fome

---

* At this period, the number of paupers in the alms-houfe
was between three and four hundred, and the managers, ap-
prehenfive of fpreading the diforder among them, enforced the
abovementioned order, which had been entered into a long

temporary place was requifite ; and three of the guardians of the poor, about the 26th of Auguft, took poffeffion of the circus, in which mr. Ricketts had lately exhibited his equeftrian feats, being the only place that could be then procured for the purpofe. Thither they fent feven perfons afflicted with the malignant fever, where they lay in the open air for fome time, and without any affiftance†. Of thefe, one crawled out on the commons, where he died at a diftance from the houfes. Two died in the circus, one of whom was feafonably removed ; the other lay in a ftate of putrefaction for above forty eight hours, owing to the difficulty of procuring any perfon to remove him. On this occafion occurred an inftance of courage in a fervant girl, of which at that time few men were capable. The carter, who finally undertook to remove the corpfe, having no affiftant, and being unable alone to put it into the coffin, was on the point of relinquifhing his defign, and quitting the place. The girl perceived him, and underftanding the difficulty he laboured under, offered her fervices, provided he would not inform the family with whom fhe lived‡. She accordingly helped him to put the body into the coffin, tho' it was, by that time, crawling with maggots, and in the moft loathfome ftate of putrefaction. It gives me pleafure to add, that fhe ftill lives, notwithftanding her very hazardous exploit.

The inhabitants of the neighbourhood of the circus took the alarm, and threatened to burn or deftroy it, unlefs the fick were removed ; and it is believed they would have actually carried their threats into execution, had compliance been delayed a day longer.

The 29th, feven of the guardians of the poor had a conference with fome of the city magiftrates on the

time before. They, however, fupplied beds and bedding, and all the money in their treafury, for their relief, out of that houfe.

† High wages were offered for nurfes for thefe poor people, —but none could be procured.

‡ Had they known of the circumftance, an immediate difmiffal would have been the confequence.

fubject of the fever, at which it was agreed to be indifpenfably neceffary, that a fuitable houfe, as an hofpital, fhould be provided near the city, for the reception of the infected poor.

In confequence, in the evening of the fame day, the guardians of the poor agreed to fundry refolutions, viz. to ufe their utmoft exertions to procure a houfe, of the above defcription, for an hofpital, (out of town, and as near thereto as might be practicable, confiftent with the fafety of the inhabitants,) for the poor who were or might be afflicted with contagious diforders, and be deftitute of the means of providing neceffary affiftance otherwife; to engage phyficians, nurfes, attendants, and all neceffaries for their relief in that houfe; to appoint proper perfons in each diftrict, to enquire after fuch poor as might be afflicted; to adminifter affiftance to them in their own houfes, and, if neceffary, to remove them to the hofpital. They referved to themfelves, at the fame time, the liberty of drawing on the mayor for fuch fums as might be neceffary to carry their plans into effect.

Conformably with thefe refolves, a committee of the guardians was appointed, to make enquiry for a fuitable place; and on due examination, they judged that a building adjacent to Bufhhill, the manfion-houfe of William Hamilton, efq. was the beft calculated for the purpofe. That gentleman was then abfent, and had no agent in the city; and the great urgency of the cafe admitting no delay, eight of the guardians, accompanied by Hilary Baker, efq. one of the city aldermen, with the concurrence of the governor, proceeded, on the 31ft of Auguft, to the building they had fixed upon; and meeting with fome oppofition from a tenant who occupied it, they took poffeffion of the manfion-houfe itfelf, to which, on the fame evening, they fent the four patients who remained at the circus.

Shortly after this, the guardians of the poor for the city, except James Wilfon, Jacob Tomkins, jun. and William Sanfom, ceafed the performance of their duties, nearly the whole of them having removed out of the city. Before this virtual vacation of office, they paſſed a reſolve againſt the admiſſion of any paupers whatever into the alms-houſe during the prevalence of the diſorder*. The whole care of the poor of the city, the providing for Buſh-hill, ſending the ſick there, and burying the dead, devolved, therefore, on the above three guardians.

C H A P. IV. *General deſpondency. Deplorable ſcenes, Frightful view of human nature. A noble and exhilarating contraſt.*

THE conſternation of the people of Philadelphia, at this period, was carried beyond all bounds. Diſmay and affright were viſible in almoſt every perſon's countenance. Moſt of thoſe who could, by any means, make it convenient, fled from the city. Of thoſe who remained, many ſhut themſelves up in their houſes, and were afraid to walk the ſtreets. The ſmoke of tobacco being regarded as a preventative, many perſons, even women and ſmall boys, had ſegars almoſt conſtantly in their mouths. Others placing full confidence in garlic, chewed it almoſt the whole day; ſome kept it in their pockets and ſhoes. Many were afraid to allow the barbers or hair-dreſſers to come near them, as inſtances had occurred of ſome of them having ſhaved the dead, and many having engaged as bleeders. Some, who carried their caution pretty far, bought lancets for themſelves, not daring to be bled with the lancets of the bleeders. Many houſes were hardly a moment in the day, free from the ſmell of gunpowder, burned tobacco, nitre, ſprinkled vinegar, &c. Some of the churches were almoſt deſerted, and others wholly cloſed. The coffee-houſe was ſhut up, as was the city library, and moſt of the public offices—three, out of the four, daily

* The reaſon for entering into this order, was, that ſome paupers, who had been admitted previous thereto, with a certificate from the phyſicians, of their being free from the infection, had, nevertheleſs, died of it.

papers were difcontinued*, as were fome of the others.
Many were almoft inceffantly employed in purifying, fcouring, and whitewafhing their rooms. Thofe
who ventured abroad, had handkerchiefs or fponges
impregnated with vinegar or camphor at their no-
fes, or fmelling-bottles full of the thieves' vinegar.
Others carried pieces of tarred rope in their hands or
pockets, or camphor bags tied round their necks.
The corpfes of the moft refpectable citizens; even of
thofe who did not die of the epidemic, were carried to the grave, on the fhafts of a chair, the horfe
driven by a negro, unattended by a friend or relation, and without any fort of ceremony. People
haftily fhifted their courfe at the fight of a hearfe
coming towards them. Many never walked on the
foot-path, but went into the middle of the ftreets,
to avoid being infected in paffing by houfes wherein
people had died. Acquaintances and friends avoided
each other in the ftreets, and only fignified their
regard by a cold nod. The old cuftom of fhaking
hands, fell into fuch general difufe, that many fhrunk
back with affright at even the offer of the hand. A
perfon with a crape, or any appearance of mourning,
was fhunned like a viper. And many valued themfelves highly on the fkill and addrefs with which they
got to windward of every perfon whom they met.
Indeed it is not probable that London, at the laft
ftage of the plague, exhibited ftronger marks of terror, than were to be feen in Philadelphia, from the
25th or 26th of Auguft, till pretty late in September. When people fummoned up refolution to walk
abroad, and take the air, the fick-cart conveying patients to the hofpital, or the hearfe carrying the
dead to the grave, which were travelling almoft the
whole day, foon damped their fpirits, and plunged
them again into defpondency.

* It would be improper to pafs over this opportunity of
mentioning, that the federal gazette, printed by Andrew
Brown, was uninterruptedly continued, and with the ufual
induftry, during the whole calamity, and was of the utmoft fervice, in conveying to the citizens of the united ftates, authentic
intelligence of the ftate of the diforder, and of the city.

While affairs were in this deplorable ſtate, and people at the loweſt ebb of deſpair, we cannot be aſtoniſhed at the frightful ſcenes that were acted, which ſeemed to indicate a total diſſolution of the bonds of ſociety in the neareſt and deareſt connexions. Who, without horror, can reflect on a huſband, married perhaps for twenty years, deſerting his wife, in the laſt agony—a wife, unfeelingly, abandoning her huſband on his death bed—parents forſaking their only children—children ungratefully flying from their parents, and reſigning them to chance, often without an enquiry after their health or ſafety—maſters hurrying off their faithful ſervants to Buſhhill, even on ſuſpicion of the fever, and that at a time, when, like Tartarus, it was open to every viſitant, but never returned any—ſervants abandoning tender and humane maſters, who only wanted a little care to reſtore them to health and uſefulneſs—who, I ſay, can think of theſe things, without horror ? Yet they were daily exhibited in every quarter of our city; and ſuch was the force of habit, that the parties who were guilty of this cruelty, felt no remorſe themſelves—nor met with the execration from their fellow-citizens, which ſuch conduct would have excited at any other period. Indeed, at this awful criſis, ſo much did *ſelf* appear to engroſs the whole attention of many, that leſs concern was felt for the loſs of a parent, a huſband, a wife, or an only child, than, on other occaſions, would have been cauſed by the death of a ſervant, or even a favourite lap-dog.

This kind of conduct produced ſcenes of diſtreſs and miſery, of which few parallels are to be met with, and which nothing could palliate, but the extraordinary public panic, and the great law of ſelf-preſervation, the dominion of which extends over the whole animated world. Many men of affluent fortunes, who have given daily employment and ſuſtenance to hundreds, have been abandoned to the care of a negro, after their wives, children, friends, clerks, and ſervants, had fled away, and left them to their fate. In many caſes, no money could procure proper attendance. With the poor, the cafe was, as might be expected, infinitely worfe than with the rich. Many of thefe have perifhed, without a human being to hand them a drink of water, to adminifter medicines, 'or to perform any charitable office for them. Various inftances have occurred, of dead bodies found lying in the ftreets, of perfons who had no houfe or habitation, and could procure no fhelter.

A man and his wife, once in affluent circumftances, were found lying dead in bed, and between them, was their child, a little infant, who was fucking its mother's breafts. How long they had lain thus, was uncertain.

A woman, whofe hufband had juft died of the fever, was feized with the pains of labour, and had nobody to affift her, as the women in the neighbourhood were afraid to go into the houfe. She lay, for a confiderable time, in a degree of anguifh that will not bear defcription. At length, fhe ftruggled to reach the window, and cried out for affiftance. Two men, paffing by, went up ftairs; but they came at too late a ftage.—She was ftriving with death—and actually, in a few minutes, expired in their arms.

Another woman, whofe hufband and two children lay dead in the room with her, was in the fame fituation as the former, without a midwife, or any other perfon to aid her. Her cries at the window brought up one of the carters employed by the committee for the relief of the fick. With his affiftance, fhe was delivered of a child, which died in a few minutes, as did the mother, who was utterly exhaufted by her labour, by the diforder, and by the dreadful fpectacle before her. And thus lay, in one room, no lefs than five dead bodies, an entire family, carried off in an hour or two. Many inftances have occurred, of refpectable women, who, in their lying-in, have been obliged to depend on their maid-fervants, for affiftance—and fome have had none but from their hufbands. Some of the midwives were dead—and others had left the city.

A fervant girl, belonging to a family in this city,

in which the fever had prevailed, was apprehenſive of danger, and reſolved to remove to a relation's houſe, in the country. She was, however, taken ſick on the road, and returned to town, where ſhe could find no perſon to receive her. One of the guardians of the poor provided a cart, and took her to the alms-houſe, into which ſhe was refuſed admittance. She was brought back, and the guardian offered five dollars to procure her a ſingle night's lodging, but in vain. And in fine, after every effort made to provide her ſhelter, ſhe abſolutely expired in the cart.

To relate all the frightful caſes of this nature that occurred, would fill a volume. To paſs them over wholly would have been improper—to dwell on them longer would be painful. Let theſe few, therefore, ſuffice. But I muſt obſerve, that moſt of them happened in the firſt ſtage of the public panic. Afterwards, when the citizens recovered a little from their fright, they became rare.

Theſe horrid circumſtances having a tendency to throw a ſhade over the human character, it is proper to reflect a little light on the ſubject, wherever juſtice and truth will permit. Amidſt the general abandonment of the ſick that prevailed, there were to be found many illuſtrious inſtances of men and women, ſome in the middle, others in the lower ſpheres of life, who, in the exerciſes of the duties of humanity, expoſed themſelves to dangers, which terrified men, who have hundreds of times faced death without fear, in the field of battle. Some of them, alas! have fallen in the good cauſe! But why ſhould they be regretted? never could they have fallen more gloriouſly. Foremoſt in this noble groupe ſtands Joſeph Inſkeep, a moſt excellent man in every of the ſocial relations of citizen, brother, huſband, and friend.— To the ſick and the forſaken has he devoted his hours, to relieve and comfort them in their tribulation, and his kind aſſiſtance was dealt out with equal freedom to an utter ſtranger as to his boſom friend. Numerous are the inſtances of men reſtored, by his kind cares and attention, to their families, from the very jaws of death.—In various cafes has he been obliged to put dead bodies into coffins, when the relations fled from the mournful office. The merit of Andrew Adgate, Joab Jones, and Daniel Offley, in the fame way, was confpicuous, and of the laft importance to numbers of diftreffed creatures, bereft of every other comfort. Of thofe worthy men, Wilfon and Tomkins, I have already fpoken. The rev. mr. Fleming and the rev. mr. Winkhaufe, exhaufted themfelves by a fucceffion of labours, day and night, attending on the fick, and miniftering relief to their fpiritual and temporal wants.

Of thofe who have happily furvived their dangers, and are preferved to their fellow citizens, I fhall mention a few. They enjoy the fupreme reward of a felf-approving confcience ; and I readily believe, that in the moft fecret receffes, remote from the public eye, they would have done the fame. But next to the fenfe of having done well, is the approbation of our friends and fellow men ; and when the debt is great, and the only payment that can be made is applaufe, it is furely the worft fpecies of avarice, to withhold it. We are always ready, too ready, alas! to beftow cenfure—and, as if anxious left we fhould not give enough, we generally heap the meafure. When we are fo folicitous to deter by reproach from folly, vice, and crime, why not be equally difpofed to ftimulate to virtue and heroifm, by freely beftowing the wellearned plaudit ? Could I fuppofe, that in any future equally-dangerous emergency, the opportunity I have feized of bearing my feeble teftimony, in favour of thefe worthy perfons, would be a means of exciting others to emulate their heroic virtue, it would afford me the higheft confolation I have ever experienced.

The rev. Henry Helmuth's merits are of the moft exalted kind. His whole time, during the prevalence of the diforder, was fpent in the performance of the works of mercy, vifiting and relieving the fick, comforting the afflicted, and feeding the hungry. Of his congregation, fome hundreds have paid the laft debt to nature, fince the malignant fever began ; and, I

believe he attended nearly the whole of them. To
fo many dangers was he expofed, that he ftands a living miracle of prefervation. The rev. C. V. Keating,
the rev. mr. Uftick, and the rev. mr. Dickens, have
been in the fame career, and performed their duties
to the fick with equal fidelity, and with equal danger. The venerable old citizen, Samuel Robefon,
has been like a good angel, indefatigably performing,
in families where there was not one perfon able to
help another, even the menial offices of the kitchen,
in every part of his neighbourhood. Thomas Allibone, Lambert Wilmer, Levi Hollingfworth, John
Barker, Hannah Paine, John Hutchinfon, and great
numbers of others have diftinguifhed themfelves by
the kindeft offices of difinterefted humanity. Magnus
Miller, Samuel Coates, and other good citizens, in
that time of pinching diftrefs and difficulty, advanced
fums of money to individuals whofe refources were
cut off, and who, though accuftomed to a life of
independence, were abfolutely deftitute of the means
of fubfiftence. And as the widow's mite has been
mentioned in fcripture with fo much applaufe, let me
add, that a worthy widow, whofe name I am griev-
ed I cannot mention, came to the city-hall, and, out of
her means, which are very moderate, offered the
committee twenty dollars for the relief of the poor.
John Connelly has fpent hours befide the fick, when
their own wives and children had abandoned them.
Twice did he catch the diforder—twice was he on the
brink of the grave, which was yawning to receive
him—yet, unappalled by the imminent danger he
had efcaped, he again returned to the charge. I feel
myfelf affected at this part of my fubject, with emotions, which I fear my unanimated ftile is ill calculated to transfufe into the breaft of my reader. I wifh
him to dwell on this part of the picture, with a degree
of exquifite pleafure equal to what I feel in the defcription. When we view man in this light, we lofe
fight of his feeblenefs, his imperfection, his vice—he
refembles, in a fmall degree, that divine being, who
is an inexhauftible mine of mercy and goodnefs.

And, as a human being, I rejoice, that it has fallen to my lot, to be a witness and recorder of a magnanimity, which would alone be sufficient to rescue the character of mortals from obloquy and reproach.

CHAP. V. *Distress increases. Benevolent citizens invited to assist the guardians of the poor. Ten volunteers. Appointment of the committee for relief of the sick. State of Philadelphia.*

IN the mean time, the situation of affairs became daily more and more serious. Those of the guardians of the poor, who continued to act, were quite oppressed with the labours of their office, which increased to such a degree, that they were utterly unable to execute them. I have already mentioned, that for the city there were but three who persevered in the performance of their duty*. It must give the reader great concern to hear, that two of them, James Wilson, and Jacob Tomkins, excellent and indefatigable young men, whose services were at that time of very great importance, fell sacrifices in the cause of humanity. The other, William Sansom, was likewise, in the execution of his dangerous office, seized with the disorder, and on the brink of the grave, but was so fortunate as to recover. The deceased persons became daily more numerous. Owing to the general terror, nurses, carters, and attendants could hardly be procured. Thus circumstanced, the mayor of the city, on the 10th of September, published an address

* With respect to the guardians of the poor, I have been misunderstood. I only spoke of those for the city. Those for the liberties, generally, continued at their post; and two of them, Wm. Peter Sprague, and William Gregory, performed, in the northern liberties, the very same kind of services as the committee did in the city, viz. attended to the burial of the dead and the removal of the sick. In Southwark, the like tour of duty was executed by Clement Humphreys, John Cornish, and Robert Jones. Far be it from me to deprive any man of applause so richly and hazardously earned. I only regret, that want of leisure prevents me from collecting the names of all those who have nobly distinguished themselves, by their attention to the alleviation of the general calamity.

to the citizens, announcing that the guardians of the poor, who remained, were in diftrefs for want of affiftance, and inviting fuch benevolent people, as felt for the general diftrefs, to lend their aid. In confequence of this advertifement, a meeting of the citizens was held at the city-hall, on Thurfday, the 12th of September, at which very few attended, from the univerfal confternation that prevailed. The ftate of the poor was fully confidered; and ten citizens, Ifrael Ifrael, Samuel Wetherill, Thomas Wiftar, Andrew Adgate, Caleb Lownes, Henry Deforeft, Thomas Peters, Jofeph Infkeep, Stephen Girard, and John Mafon, offered themfelves to affift the guardians of the poor. At this meeting, a committee was appointed to confer with the phyficians who had the care of Bufh-hill, and make report of the ftate of that hofpital. This committee reported next evening, that it was in very bad order, and in want of almoft every thing.

On Saturday, the 14th, another meeting was held, when the alarming ftate of affairs being fully confidered, it was refolved to borrow fifteen hundred dollars of the bank of North-America, for the purpofe of procuring fuitable accommodations for the ufe of perfons afflicted with the prevailing malignant fever. At this meeting, a committee was appointed to tranfact the whole of the bufinefs relative to the relief of the fick, and the procuring of phyficians, nurfes, attendants, &c. This is the committee, which, by virtue of that appointment, has, from that day to the prefent time, watched over the fick, the poor, the widow, and the orphan. It is worthy of remark, and may encourage others in time of public calamity, that this committee confifted originally of only twenty-fix perfons, men moftly taken from the middle walks of life; of thefe, four, Andrew Adgate, Jonathan Dickinfon Sargeant, Daniel Offley, and Jofeph Infkeep, died, the two firft at an early period of their labours—and four never attended to the appointment. " The heat and burden of the day" have therefore been borne by eighteen perfons, whofe exertions have been so highly favoured by providence, that they have been the instruments of averting the progress of destruction, eminently relieving the distressed, and restoring confidence to the terrified inhabitants of Philadelphia. It is honourable to this committee, that they have conducted their business with more harmony than is generally to be met with in public bodies of equal number. Probably there never was one, of which the members were so regular in their attendance ; the meetings, at the worst of times—those times, which, to use Paine's emphatic language, " tried men's souls," were composed in general, of twelve, thirteen, and fourteen members.

Never, perhaps, was there a city in the situation of Philadelphia at this period: The president of the united states, according to his annual custom, had removed to Mount Vernon with his household. Most, if not all of the other officers of the federal government were absent. The governor, who had been sick, had gone, by directions of his physician, to his country-seat near the falls of Schuylkill—and nearly the whole of the officers of the state had likewise retired.—The magistrates of the city, except the mayor*, and John Barclay†, esq. were away, as were most of those of the liberties. Of the situation of the guardians of the poor‡, I have already made mention. In fact, government of every kind was almost wholly vacated, and seemed, by tacit, but universal consent, to be vested in the committee.

* This magistrate deserves particular praise. He was the first who invited the citizens to " rally round the standard" of charity, and convened the meeting at which the committee for relief of the sick was appointed, as well as the preceding ones ; of this committee he was appointed president, and punctually fulfilled his duty during the whole time of the distress.

† This gentleman, late mayor of the city, acted in the double capacity of alderman and president of the bank of Pennsylvania, to the duties of which offices he devoted himself unremittedly, except during an illness which threatened to add him to the number of valuable men of whom we have been bereft.

‡ The managers of the alms-house attended to the duties imposed on them, and met regularly at that building every week.

CHAP. VI. *Magnanimous offer. Wretched state of Bush-hill. Order introduced there.*

AT the meeting on Sept. 15th, a circumstance oc-curred, to which the most glowing pencil could hardly do justice. Stephen Girard, a wealthy merchant, a native of France, and one of the members of the committee, touched with the wretched situation of the sufferers at Bush-hill, voluntarily and unexpect-edly offered himself as a manager, to superintend that hospital. The surprize and satisfaction, excited by this extraordinary effort of humanity, can be better conceived than expressed. Peter Helm, a native of Pennsylvania, also a member, actuated by the like benevolent motives, offered his services in the same department, Their offers were accepted ; and the same afternoon they entered on the execution of their dangerous and praise-worthy office*.

To form a just estimate of the value of the offer of these men, it is necessary to take into full considera-tion the general consternation, which at that period pervaded every quarter of the city, and which made attendance on the sick be regarded as little less than a certain sacrifice. Uninfluenced by any reflexions of this kind, without any possible inducement but the purest motives of humanity, they came forward and offered themselves as the forlorn hope of the committee. I trust that the gratitude of their fellow-citizens will remain as long as the memory of their beneficent conduct, which I hope will not die with the present generation.

On the 16th, the managers of Bush-hill, after per-sonal inspection of the state of affairs there, made report of its situation, which was truly deplorable. It exhibited as wretched a picture of human misery as ever existed. A profligate, abandoned set of nurses and attendants (hardly any of good character could at that time be procured,) rioted on the provi-sions and comforts prepared for the sick, who

* The management of the interior department was assumed by Stephen Girard—the exterior by Peter Helm.

(unless at the hours when the doctors attended)
were left almost entirely destitute of every assistance.
The sick, the dying, and the dead were indiscriminately mingled together. The ordure and other evacuati-
ons of the sick, were allowed to remain in the
most offensive state imaginable. Not the smallest appearance of order or regularity existed. It was, in
fact, a great human slaughter-house, where numerous victims were immolated at the altar of riot
and intemperance. No wonder, then, that a general dread of the place prevailed through the city, and
that a removal to it was considered as the seal of
death. In consequence, there were various instances
of sick persons locking their rooms, and resisting
every attempt to carry them away. At length, the
poor were so much afraid of being sent to Bush-hill,
that they would not acknowledge their illness, until it
was no longer possible to conceal it. For it is to be
observed, that the fear of the contagion was so prevalent, that as soon as any one was taken ill, an alarm
was spread among the neighbours, and every effort
was used to have the sick person hurried off to Bush-
hill, to avoid spreading the disorder. The cases of
poor people forced in this way to that hospital, though
labouring under only common colds, and common
fall fevers, were numerous and afflicting. There were
not wanting instances of persons, only slightly ill,
being sent to Bush-hill, by their panic-struck neighbours, and embracing the first opportunity of running back to Philadelphia.

The regulations adopted at Bush-hill, were as
follow :

One of the rooms in the mansion house (which
contains fourteen, besides three large entries) was
allotted to the matron, and an assistant under her—
eleven rooms and two entries to the sick. Those who
were in a very low state were in one room—and one
was appointed for the dying. The men and women
were kept in distinct rooms, and attended by nurses
of their own sexes. Every sick person was furnished
with a bedstead, clean sheet, pillow, two or three blan-

kets, perringer, plate, fpoon, and clean linen, when neceffary. In the manfion houfe were one hundred and forty bedfteads. The new frame houfe, built by the committee, when it was found that the old buildings were inadequate to contain the patients commodioufly, is fixty feet front, and eighteen feet deep, with three rooms on the ground floor; one of which was for the head nurfes of that houfe, the two others for the fick. Each of thefe two laft contained feventeen bedfteads. The loft, defigned for the convalefcents, was calculated to contain forty.

The barn is a large, commodious ftone building, divided into three apartments; one occupied by the refident doctors and apothecary; one, which contained forty bedfteads, by the men convalefcents—and the other by the women convalefcents, which contained fifty-feven.

At fome diftance from the weft of the hofpital, was erected a frame building to ftore the coffins, and depofite the dead until they were fent to a place of interment.

Befides the nurfes employed in the houfe, there were two cooks, four labourers, and three wafherwomen, conftantly employed for the ufe of the hofpital.

The fick were vifited twice a day by two phyficians, dr. Devezé and dr. Benjamin Duffield*, whofe prefcriptions were executed by three refident phyficians and the apothecary.

One of the refident doctors was charged with the diftribution of the victuals for the fick. At eleven o'clock, he gave them broth with rice, bread, boiled

---

* Very foon after the organization of the committee; dr. Devezé, a refpectable French phyfician from Cape-Francois, offered his fervices in the line of his profeffion at Bufh-hill. Dr. Benjamin Duffield did the fame. Their offers were accepted; and they have both attended with great punctuality. Dr. Deveze renounced all other practice, which, at that period, would have been very lucrative, when there was fuch general demand for phyficians. The committee, in confideration of the fervices of thefe two gentlemen, have lately prefented dr. Duffield with five hundred, and dr. Deveze with fifteen hundred dollars.

E

beef, veal, mutton, and chicken, with cream of rice to thofe whofe ftomachs would not bear ftronger nourifhment. Their fecond meal was at fix o'clock, when they had broth, rice, boiled prunes, with cream of rice; The fick drank at their meals porter, or claret and water. Their conftant drink between meals was centaury tea, and boiled lemonade.

Thefe regulations, the order and regularity introduced, and the care and tendernefs with which the patients, were treated, foon eftablifhed the character of the hofpital ; and in the courfe of a week or two, numbers of fick people, who had not at home proper perfons to nurfe them, applied to be fent to Bufh-hill. Indeed, in the end, fo many people, who were afflicted with other diforders, procured admittance there, that it became neceffary to pafs a refolve, that before an order of admiffion fhould be granted, a certificate muft be produced from a phyfician, that the patient laboured under the malignant fever ; for had all the applicants been received, this hofpital, provided for an extraordinary occafion, would have been filled with patients whofe cafes entitled them to a reception in the Pennfylvania hofpital.

The number of perfons received into Bufh-hill, from the 16th of September to this time, is about one thoufand ; of whom nearly five hundred are dead; there are now (Nov. 30,) in the houfe, about twenty fick, and fifty convalefcents. Of the latter clafs, there have been difmiffed about four hundred and thirty.

The reafon why fo large a proportion died of thofe received, is, that in a variety of cafes, the early fears of that hofpital had got fuch firm poffeffion of the minds of fome, and others were fo much actuated by a foolifh pride, that they would never confent to be removed till they were paft recovery. And in confequence of this, there were many inftances of perfons dying in the cart on the road to the hofpital. I fpeak within bounds, when I fay that at leaft a third of the whole number of thofe received, did not furvive their entrance into the hofpital two days. Were it not for the operation of thefe two motives, the number of the dead in the city and in the hospital would have been much lessened; for many a man, whose nice feelings made him spurn at the idea of a removal to the hospital, perished in the city for want of that comfortable assistance he would have had at Bush-hill*.

Before I conclude this chapter, let me add, that the perseverance of the managers of that hospital has been equally meritorious with their original beneficence. During the whole calamity to this time, they have attended uninterruptedly, for six, seven, or eight hours a day, renouncing almost every care of private affairs. They have had a laborious tour of duty to perform. Stephen Girard, whose office was in the interior part of the hospital, has had to encourage and comfort the sick—to hand them necessaries and medicines—to wipe the sweat off their brows—and to perform many disgusting offices of kindness for them; which nothing could render tolerable, but the exalted motives that impelled him to this heroic conduct. Peter Helm, his worthy coadjutor, displayed, in his department, equal exertions, to promote the common good.

CHAP. VII. *Proceedings of the committee—Loans from the bank of North-America. Establishment of an orphan-house. Relief of the poor. Appointment of the assistant committee.*

THE committee, on its organization, resolved that three of the members should attend daily at the city hall, to receive applications for relief; to provide for the burial of the dead, and for the convey-

---

* I omitted in the former editions to mention the name of a most excellent and invaluable woman, mrs. Saville, the matron in this hospital, whose services in the execution of her office, were above all price. Never was there a person better qualified for such a situation. To the most strict observance of system, she united all the tenderness and humanity which are so essentially requisite in an hospital, but which habit so very frequently and fatally extinguishes: should the wisdom of our legislature decree the permanent establishment of a lazaretto, no person can be found more deserving, or better qualified to be entrusted with the care of it.

ance of perfons labouring uuder the malignant fever, to Bufh-hill. But three being found inadequate to the execution of the multifarious and laborious duties to be performed, this order was refcinded, and daily attendance was given by nearly all of the members.

. A number of carts and carters were engaged for the burial of the dead, and removal of the fick. And it was a melancholy fight to behold them inceffantly employed through the whole day, in thefe mournful offices.

The committee borrowed fifteen hundred dollars from the bank of North-America, agreeably to the refolves of the town meeting by which they were appointed. Several of the members entered into fecurity to repay that fum, in cafe the corporation or legiflature fhould refufe to make provifion for its difcharge. This fum being foon expended, a farther loan of five thoufand dollars was negociated with the fame inftitution*.

In the progrefs of the diforder, the committee found the calls on their humanity increafe. The numerous deaths of heads of families left a very large body of children in a moft abandoned, forlorn ftate. The bettering houfe, in which fuch helplefs objects have been ufually placed heretofore, was barred againft them, by the order which I have already mentioned. Many of thefe little innocents were actually fuffering for want of even common neceffaries. The deaths of their parents and protectors, which ' fhould have been the ftrongeft recommendation to public charity, was the very reafon of . their diftrefs, and of their being fhunned as a peftilence. The children of a family once in eafy circumftances, were found in a blackfmith's fhop, fqualid, dirty, and half ftarved, having been for a confiderable time without even bread to eat. Various inftances of a fimilar nature occurred. This evil early caught the attention of the committee, and on the 19th of September, they hired a houfe in

---

* It ought to be mentioned, that on the payment of thefe fums, the directors genproufly declined accepting intereft for the ufe of them.

Fifth-ftreet, in which they placed thirteen children.
The number increafing, they on the 3d of October,
procured the Loganian library, which was generoufly
given up by John Swanwick, efq. for the purpofe of
an orphan houfe. A further increafe of their little
charge, rendered it neceffary to build fome additions
to the library, which are nearly half as large as that
building.' At prefent, there are in the houfe, under
the care of the orphan committee, about fixty children, and above forty are out with wet nurfes.
From the origin of the inflitution, one hundred and
ninety children have fallen under their care, of whom
fixteen are dead, and about feventy have been delivered to their relations or friends. There are inftances
of five and fix children of a fingle family in the houfe.

To thefe precious depofits the utmoft attention has
been paid. They are well fed, comfortably clothed,
and properly taken care of. Mary Parvin, a very fuitable perfon for the purpofe, has been engaged as
matron, and there are, befides, fufficient perfons employed to affift her. Various applications have been
made for fome of the children; but in no inftance
would the committee furrender any of them up, until
they had fatisfactory evidence that the claimants had
a right to make the demand. Their relations are now
publicly called upon to come and receive them. For
fuch as may remain unclaimed, the beft provifion poffible will be made; and fo great is the avidity of many
people to have fome of them, that there will be no
difficulty in placing them to advantage.

Another duty foon attracted the attention of the
committee. The flight of fo many of our citizens, the
confequent ftagnation of bufinefs, and the almoft total
ceffation of the labours of the guardians of the poor,
brought on among the lower claffes of the people, a
great degree of diftrefs, which loudly demanded the in-
terpofition of the humane. In confequence, on the 20th
of September, a committee of diftribution, of three
members, was appointed, to furnifh fuch affiftance to
deferving objects as their refpective cafes might require, and the funds allow. This was at firft adminif-

tered to but few, owing to the confined ſtate of the finances. But the very extraordinary liberality of our fugitive fellow citizens, of the citizens of New York, and of thoſe of various towns and townſhips, encouraged the committee to extend their views. In conſequence, they increaſed the diſtributing committee to eight, and afterwards to ten.

Being, in the execution of this important ſervice, liable to impoſition, they, on the 14th of October, appointed an aſſiſtant committee, compoſed of forty-five citizens, choſen from the ſeveral diſtricts of the city and liberties. The duty aſſigned this aſſiſtant committee, was to ſeek out and give recommendations to deſerving objects in diſtreſs, who, on producing them, were relieved by the committee of diſtribution, (who ſat daily at the City Hall, in rotation,) with money, proviſions, or wood, or all three, according as their neceſſities required. The aſſiſtant committee executed this buſineſs with ſuch care, that it is probable ſo great a number of people were never before relieved, with ſo little impoſition. Some ſhameleſs creatures, poſſeſſed of houſes, and comfortable means of ſupport, have been detected in endeavouring to partake of the relief deſtined ſolely for the really indigent and diſtreſſed.

Beſides thoſe who came forward to aſk aſſiſtance in the way of gift, there was another claſs, in equal diſtreſs, and equally entitled to relief, who could not deſcend to accept it as charity. The committee, diſpoſed to foſter this laudable principle, one of the beſt ſecurities from debaſement of character, relieved perſons of this deſcription with ſmall loans weekly, juſt enough for immediate ſupport, and took acknowledgments for the debt, without ever intending to urge payment, if not perfectly convenient to the parties.

The number of perſons relieved weekly, was about twelve hundred ; many of whom had families of four, five, and ſix perſons.

The gradual revival of buſineſs has reſcued thoſe who are able and willing to work, from the humiliation of depending on public charity. And the organization of the overſeers of the poor has thrown the

fupport of the proper objects of charity into its old
channel. The diftribution of money, &c. ceafed therefore on Saturday, the 23d of November.

C H A P. VIII. *Repeated addreffes of the committee on
the purification of houfes.—Affiftant committee undertake to infpect infected houfes perfonally. Extinction
of the diforder. Governor's proclamation. Addrefs of the
clergy. A new and happy ftate of affairs.*

THE committee exerted its cares for the welfare
of the citizens in every cafe in which its interference was at all proper or neceffary. The declenfion of
the diforder induced many perfons to return to the
city at an earlier period, than prudence dictated. On
the 26th of October, therefore, the committee addreffed their fellow citizens, congratulating them on the
very flattering change that had taken place, which afforded a chearing profpect of being foon freed from
the diforder entirely. They, however, recommended
to thofe who were abfent, not to return till the inter-
vention of cold weather, or rain* fhould render fuch
a ftep juftifiable and proper, by totally extinguifhing
the difeafe.

The 29th, they publifhed another addrefs, earneftly
exhorting thofe whofe houfes had been clofed, to have
them well aired and purified; to throw lime into the
privies, &c.

The 4th of November, they again addreffed the
public, announcing that it was unfafe for thofe who
had refided in the country, to return to town with too
much precipitation, efpecially into houfes not properly
prepared. They added, that though the diforder had
confiderably abated, and though there was reafon to
hope it would fhortly difappear, yet they could not
fay it was totally eradicated; as there was reafon to
fear it ftill lurked in different parts of the city. They
reiterated their reprefentations on the fubject of
cleanfing houfes.

* I fhall in fome of the following pages attempt to prove, that
the idea here held out, was erroneous.

The 14th, they once more addreſſed their fellow citizens, informing them of the reſtoration to our long afflicted city, of as great a degree of health as uſually prevails at the ſame ſeaſon ; of no new caſes of the malignant fever having occurred for many days; of their having reaſon to hope that in a few days not a veſtige of it would remain in the city or ſuburbs; of applications for admiſſion into the hoſpital having ceaſed ; of the expectation of the phyſicians at the hoſpital, that no more than three or four would die out of ninety-one perſons remaining there ; of the number of convaleſcents increaſing daily. They at the ſame time moſt earneſtly recommended that houſes in which the diſorder had been, ſhould be purified ; and that the clothing or bedding of the ſick, more eſpecially of thoſe who had died of the diſorder, ſhould be waſhed, baked, buried, or deſtroyed. They added, that the abſent citizens of Philadelphia, as well as thoſe ſtrangers who had buſineſs in the city, might ſafely come to it, without fear of the diſorder.

Notwithſtanding all theſe cautions, many perſons returned from the country, without paying any attention to the cleanſing of their houſes, thereby ſporting not only with their own lives, but with the ſafety of their fellow citizens. The neglect of ſome people, in this way, has been ſo flagrant, as to merit the ſevereſt puniſhment. This dangerous nuiſance attracted the notice of the committee ; and after a conference with the aſſiſtant committee, they, on the 15th of November, in conjunction with them, reſolved, that it was highly expedient to have all houſes and ſtores in the city and liberties, wherein the malignant fever had prevailed, purified and cleanſed as ſpeedily and completely as poſſible ; to have all thoſe well aired, which had been cloſed for any length of time ; to have lime thrown into the privies ; to call in, when the diſtrict ſhould be too large for the members to enforce compliance with thoſe reſolves, ſuch aſſiſtants as might be neceſſary ; and when any perſon, whoſe houſe required to be cleanſed, and who was able to defray the expenſe thereof, ſhould refuſe or neglect to comply with the requifition of the members appointed to carry thofe refolves into effect, to report him to the next grand jury for the city and county, as fupporting a nuifance dangerous to the public welfare. The affif-tant committee undertook to exert themfelves to have thefe falutary plans put into execution; they have gone through the city and liberties for the purpofe; and in moft cafes have found a readinefs in the inha-bitants to comply with a requifition of fuch impor-tance*.

This was the laft act of the committee that re-quires notice. Their bufinefs has fince gone on in a regular, uniform train, every day like the paft. They are now fettling their accounts, and are prepar-ing to furrender up their truft, into the hands of a town meeting of their fellow citizens, the conftitu-ents by whom they were called into the unprece-dented office they have filled. To them they will give an account of their ftewardfhip, in a time of diftrefs, the like of which heaven avert from the people of America for ever. Doubtlefs, a candid conftruction will be put upon their conduct, and it will be believed, that they have acted in every cafe that came under their cognizance, according to the beft of their abi-lities.

On the 14th, governor Mifflin publifhed a procla-mation, announcing, that as it had pleafed Almighty God to put an end to the grievous calamity which recently afflicted the city of Philadelphia, it was the duty of all who were truly fenfible of the divine mercy, to employ the earlieft moments of returning health, in devout expreffions of penitence, fubmiffion, and gratitude. He therefore appointed Thurfday, the

---

* The utmoft exertions of the magiftrates, and of the citizens generally, are neceffary to guard againft the deplorable confe-quences that may arife in the fpring from the neglect of a few, whofe fupinenefs renders them deaf to every call of duty in this refpect. The beds fecreted by the nurfes who attended the fick, are likewife a fruitful fource of danger, and demand the greateft vigilance from every perfon invefted with authority to watch over the public fafety.

F

12th of December†, as a day of general humiliation, thankſgiving, and prayer, and earneſtly exhorted and intreated his fellow citizens " to abſtain, on that day, from all worldly avocations, and to unite in confeſſing, with contrite hearts, their manifold ſins and tranſgreſſions—in acknowledging, with thankful adoration, the mercy and goodneſs of the Supreme Ruler of the univerſe, more eſpecially manifeſted in our late deliverance; and in praying, with ſolemn zeal, that the ſame mighty power would be graciouſly pleaſed to inſtil into our minds the juſt principles of our duty to him and to our fellow creatures; to regulate and guide all our actions by his Holy Spirit, to avert from all mankind the evils of war, peſtilence, and famine; and to bleſs and protect us in the enjoyment of civil and religious liberty."

The 18th, the clergy of the city publiſhed an elegant and pathetic addreſs, recommending that the day appointed by the governor, " ſhould be ſet apart and kept holy to the Lord, not merely as a day of thankſgiving, for that, in all appearance, it had pleaſed him, of his infinite mercy, to ſtay the rage of the malignant diſorder, (when we had well nigh ſaid, hath God forgot to be gracious?)—but alſo as a day of ſolemn humiliation and prayer, joined with the confeſſion of our manifold ſins, and of our neglect and abuſe of his former mercies; together with ſincere reſolutions of future amendment and obedience to his holy will and laws; without which our prayers, praiſes, and thankſgivings will be in vain."

The 26th the aſſiſtant committee paſſed ſeveral very judicious and ſalutary reſolves, requiring their members in their ſeveral diſtricts through the city and liberties, immediately to inſpect the condition of all taverns, boarding houſes, and other buildings

† The pious obſervance of this day, by an almoſt total ceſſation of buſineſs (except among the Friends, whoſe ſtores generally remained open) and by the churches being univerſally filled with people pouring forth the effuſions of their gratitude for the ceſſation of the dreadful ſcourge, exceeded that of any other day of thankſgiving I have ever known.

in which the late contagious diforder is known to have been ; to notify the owners or tenants, to have them purified and cleanfed ; to report the names of fuch as fhould refufe compliance, and alfo make report of every houfe fhut up, in which any perfon is known to have lately fickened or died. They caution-ed the vendue mafters not to fell, and the public not to buy any clothes or bedding belonging to perfons lately deceafed, until they know that the fame has been fufficiently purified and aired.

I have not judged it neceffary to enter into a minute detail of the bufinefs of the committee from day to day. It would afford little gratification to the reader. It would be, for feveral weeks, little more than a melan-choly biflory of fifteen, twenty, or thirty applications daily, for coffins and carts to bury the dead, who had none to perform that laft office for them—or as many applications for the removal of the fick to Bufh hill. There was little variety. The prefent day was as drea-ry as the paft—and the profpect of the approaching one was equally gloomy. This was the flate of things for a long time. But at length brighter profpects dawned. The diforder decreafed in violence. The number of the fick diminifhed. New cafes became rare. The fpirits of the citizens revived—and the tide of migration was once more turned. A vifible alteration has taken place in the flate of affairs in the city. Our friends return in crouds. Every hour, long-abfent and welcome faces appear—and in many inftances, thofe of perfons, whom public fame has buried for weeks paft. The ftores, fo long clofed, are nearly all opened again. Many of the country merchants, bolder than others, are daily venturing in to their old place of fupply. Mar-ket-ftreet is as full of waggons as ufual. The cuftom-houfe, for weeks nearly deferted by our mercantile people, is thronged with citizens entering their veffels and goods. The ftreets, too long the abode of gloom and defpair, have affumed the buftle fuited to the fea-fon. Our wharves are filled with veffels loading and unloading their refpective cargoes. And, in fine, as every thing, in the early ſtage of the diſorder, ſeemed calculated to add to the general conſternation; ſo now, on the contrary, every circumſtance has a tendency to revive the courage and hopes of our citizens. But we have to lament, that the ſame ſpirit of exaggeration and lying, that prevailed at a former period, and was the grand cauſe of the harſh meaſures adopted by our ſiſter ſtates, has not ceaſed to operate; for at the preſent moment, when the danger is entirely done away, the credulous, of our own citizens ſtill abſent, and of the country people, are ſtill alarmed with frightful rumours, of the diſorder raging with as much violence as ever; of numbers carried off, a few hours after their return; and of new caſes daily occurring. To what deſign to attribute theſe ſhameful tales, I know not. Were I to regard them in a ſpirit of reſentment, I ſhould be inclined to charge them to ſome ſecret, intereſted views of their authors, intent, if poſſible, to effect the entire deſtruction of our city. But I will not allow myſelf to conſider them in this point of light—and will even ſuppoſe they ariſe from a pronenefs to terrific narration, natural to ſome men. But they ſhould conſider, that we are in the ſituation of the frogs in the fable—while thoſe tales, which make the hair of the country people ſtand on end, are ſport to the fabricators, they are death to us. And I here aſſert, and defy contradiction, that of the whole number of our fugitive citizens, who have already returned, amounting to ſome thouſands, not above two perſons are dead—and theſe owe their fate to the moſt ſhameful neglect of airing and cleanſing their houſes, notwithſtanding the various cautions publiſhed by the committee. If people will venture into houſes in which infected air has been pent up for weeks together, without any purification, we cannot be ſurprized at the conſequences, however fatal they may be. But let not the cataſtrophe of a few incautious perſons operate to bring diſcredit on a city containing above fifty thouſand people.

CHAP. IX. *Extravagant letters from Philadelphia. Credulity put to the test.*

THAT I might not interrupt the chain of events in Philadelphia, I have deferred, till now, giving an account of the proceedings in the several states, respecting our fugitives. As an introduction thereto, I shall prefix a short chapter respecting those letters, which excited the terror of our neighbours, and impelled them to more severe measures than they would otherwise have adopted.

Great as was the calamity of Philadelphia, it was magnified in the most extraordinary manner. The hundred tongues of rumour were never more successfully employed, than on this melancholy occasion. The terror of the inhabitants of all the neighbouring states was excited by letters from this city, distributed by every mail, many of which told tales of woe, whereof hardly a single circumstance was true, but which were every where received with implicit faith. The distresses of the city, and the fatality of the disorder, were exaggerated as it were to see how far credulity could be carried. The plague of London was, according to rumour, hardly more fatal than our yellow fever. Our citizens died so fast, that there was hardly enough of people to bury them. Ten, or fifteen, *or more*, were said to be cast into one hole together, like so many dead beasts*. One man, whose feelings were so composed, as to be facetious on the subject, ac-

---

* The following extract appeared in a Norfolk paper about the middle of September:

Extract of a letter from Philadelphia, to a gentleman in Norfolk, Sept. 9.

" Half the inhabitants of this city have already fled to different " parts, on account of the pestilential disorder that prevails here. " The few citizens who remained in this place, die in abundance, " *so fast, that they drag them away, like dead beasts, and put ten,* " *or fifteen, or more, in a hole together. All the stores are shut up.* " I am afraid this city will be ruined: for nobody will come near " it hereafter. I am this day removing my family from this fatal " place." I am strongly inclined to imagine that this letter was the cause of the Virginia proclamation.

quainted a correfpondent, in New York, that the
only bufinefs carrying on, was *grave digging*, or rather *pit digging* †.   And at a time when the deaths did
not exceed from forty to fifty daily, many men had
the modefty to write, and others, throughout the con-
tinent, the credulity to believe, that we buried from one
hundred to one hundred and fifty*.   Thoufands were
fwept off in three or four weeks ‡.   And the nature

† *From a New York paper of October* 2.

Extract of a letter from a gentleman in Philadelphia, dated Sept. 23.

"The papers muft have amply informed you of the melancho-
"ly fituation of this city for five or fix weeks paft. *Grave-dig-*
"*ging* has been the only bufinefs carrying on ; and indeed I may
"fay of late, *pit-digging,* where people are interred indifcrimi-
"nately in three tiers of coffins. From the moft accurate ob-
"fervations I can make upon matters, I think I fpeak with-
"in bounds, when I fay, eighteen hundred perfons have perifhed
"(I do not fay all of the yellow fever) fince its firft appearance."

* *From the Maryland Journal, of Sept.* 27.

Extract of a letter from Philadelphia, dated Sept. 20.

"The diforder feems to be much the fame in this place as
"when I laft wrote you : about 1500 have fallen victims to it.
"Laft Sunday, Monday, and Tuefday, there were not lefs than
"350 died with this fevere diforder !!! As I informed you be-
"fore, this is the moft diftreffed place I ever beheld. Whole fa-
"milies go in the diforder, in the courfe of twelve hours. For
"your own fakes, ufe all poffible means to keep it out of Balti-
"more."

Extract of a letter from Philadelphia, of the fame date.

"The malignant fever which prevails here, is ftill increaf-
"ing. Report fays, that above one hundred have been buried
"per day for fome time paft. It is now thought to be more in-
"fectious than ever. I think you ought to be very careful with
"refpect to admitting perfons from Philadelphia into your town."

‡ *From a Cheftertown paper, of Sept.* 10.

Extract of a letter from a refpectable young mechanic, in Philadel-
phia, to his friend in this town, dated the 5th inft.

"It is now a very mortal time in this city. The yellow fever
"hath *killed fome thoufands* of the inhabitants. Eight thoufand
"mechanics, befides other people, have left the town. Every
"mafter in the city, of our branch of bufinefs, is gone." The
"*fome thoufands*" that were *killed* at that time, did not amount
to three hundred. The *authentic* information in this letter, was

and danger of the diforder, were as much mifrepre-
fented, as the number of the dead. It was faid, in defiance of every day's experience, to be as inevitable by
all expofed to the contagion, as the ftroke of fate.

The credulity of fome, the pronenefs to exaggeration of others, and I am forry, extremely forry to believe, the interefted views of a few*, will account for
thefe letters.

CHAP. X. *Proceedings at Cheftertown—At New-York
—At Trenton and Lamberton—At Baltimore.*

THE effects produced by thofe tales, were fuch
as might be reafonably expected. The confternation fpread through the feveral ftates like wild-fire.
The firft public act that took place on the fubject, as
far as I can learn, was at Cheftertown, in Maryland.
At this place, a meeting was held on the 10th of September, and feveral refolves entered into, which, after
fpecifying that the diforder had extended to Trenton,
Princeton, Woodbridge, and Elizabeth-town, on the
poft-road to New-York, directed, that notice fhould
be fent to the owners of the ftages not to allow them
to pafs through the town, while there fhould be reafon
to expect danger therefrom; and that a committee of
health and infpection fhould be appointed, to provide
for the relief of fuch poor inhabitants as might take
the diforder, and likewife for fuch ftrangers as might
be infected with it. In confequence of thefe refolves,
the eaftern fhore line of ftages was ftopt in the courfe
of a few days afterwards.

The alarm in New-York was firft officially an-
nounced by a letter from the mayor to the practifing

circulated in every ftate in the union, by the news papers. From
the date, I fufpect this letter to have been the occafion of the
Cheftertown refolves.

* As this charge is extremely pointed, it may be requifite to
ftate the foundation of it, for the reader to form his opinion upon.
Some of the letters from Philadelphia about this time, were written by perfons, whofe intereft it was to injure the city; and gave
ftatements fo very different, even from the very worft rumours
prevailing here, that it was morally impoffible the writers themfelves could have believed them.

phyſicians, dated Sept. 11th, in which he requeſted them to report to him in writing the names of all ſuch perſons as had arrived; or ſhould arrive from Philadelphia, or any other place, by land or water, and were or ſhould be ſick; and that ſuch as ſhould be deemed ſubjects of infectious diſeaſes, might be removed out of the city. He notified them, that the corporation had taken meaſures to provide a proper place as an hoſpital, for ſuch perſons as might unhappily become ſubjects of the fever in New-York. In this letter the mayor declared his opinion clearly, that the intercourſe with Philadelphia, could not be lawfully interrupted by any power in the ſtate. The 12th appeared a proclamation from governor Clinton, which, referring to the " act to prevent the bringing in, and " ſpreading of infectious diſorders," prohibited, in the terms of that act, all veſſels from Philadelphia, to approach nearer to the city of New-York, than Bedlow's iſland, about two miles diſtant, till duly diſcharged. The ſilence of this proclamation, reſpecting paſſengers by land, ſeemed to imply that the governor's opinion on the ſubject, was the ſame as that of the mayor.

The ſame day, at a meeting of the citizens, the neceſſity of taking ſome precautions was unanimouſly agreed upon, and a committee of ſeven appointed to report a plan to a meeting to be held next day. Their report, which was unanimouſly agreed to, the 13th, recommended to hire two phyſicians, to aſſiſt the phyſician of the port in his examination of veſſels; to check, as much as poſſible, the intercourſe by ſtages; to acquaint the proprieters of the ſouthern ſtages, that it was the earneſt wiſh of the inhabitants, that their carriages and boats ſhould not paſs during the prevalence of the diſorder in Philadelphia; and to requeſt the practioners of phyſic to report, without fail, every caſe of fever, to which they might be called, occurring in any perſon that had or might arrive from Philadelphia, or have intercourſe with them. Not ſatisfied with theſe meaſures, the corporation, on the 17th, came to reſolution to ſtop all intercourſe between the two cities; and for this purpose guards were placed at the different landings, with orders to send back every person coming from Philadelphia; and if any were discovered to have arrived after that date, they were to be directly sent back. Those who took in lodgers, were called upon to give information of all people of the above description, under pain of being prosecuted according to law. All good citizens were required to give information to the mayor, or any member of the committee, of any breach in the premises.

These strict precautions being eluded by the fears and the vigilance of the fugitives from Philadelphia, on the 23d there was a meeting held, of delegates from the several wards of the city, in order to adopt more effectual measures. At this meeting, it was resolved to establish a night watch of not less than ten citizens in each ward, to guard against every attempt to enter under cover of darkness. Not yet eased of their fears, they next day published an address, in which they mentioned, that notwithstanding their utmost vigilance many persons had been clandestinely landed upon the shores of New-York island. They therefore again called upon their fellow citizens to be cautious how they received strangers into their houses; not to fail to report all such to the mayor immediately upon their arrival; to remember the importance of the occasion; and to consider what reply they should make to the just resentment of their fellow citizens, whose lives they might expose by a criminal neglect, or infidelity. They likewise declared their expectation, that those who kept the different ferries on the shores of New-Jersey and Staten island, would pay such attention to their address, as not to transport any person but to the public landings, and that in the day time, between sun and sun. The 30th they published a lengthy address, recapitulating the various precautions they had taken—the nature of the disorder—and the numbers who had died out of Philadelphia, without communicating it to any one. They at the same time resolved, that goods, bedding, and

G

clothing, packed up in Philadelphia, ſhould, pré-
vious to their being brought into New-York, be un-
packed and expoſed to the open air in ſome well
ventilated place, for at leaſt 48 hours; that all linen
or cotton clothes, or bedding, which had been uſed,
ſhould be well waſhed in ſeveral waters; and afterwards, that the whole, both ſuch as had been and
ſuch as had not been uſed, ſhould be hung up in a
cloſe room, and well ſmoked with the fumes of brim-
ſtone for one day, and after that again expoſed for
at leaſt twenty four hours to the open air; and that
the boxes, trunks, or cheſts, in which they had been
packed, ſhould be cleaned and aired in the ſame manner; after which, being repacked, and ſuch evidence
given of their purification, as the committee ſhould
require, permiſſion might be had to bring them into
the city.

The 11th of October, they likewiſe reſolved, that
they would conſider and publiſh to the world, as ene-
mies to the welfare of the city, and the lives of its inhabitants, all thoſe who ſhould be ſo ſelfiſh and hardy,
as to attempt to introduce any goods, wares, merchandize, bedding, baggage, &c. imported from, or
packed up in Philadelphia, contrary to the rules pre-
ſcribed by that body, who were, they ſaid, deputed
to expreſs the will of their fellow citizens. They
recommended to the inhabitants to withſtand any
temptation of profit, which might attend the purchaſe
of goods in Philadelphia, as no emolument to an in-
dividual, they added, could warrant the hazard to
which ſuch conduct might expoſe the city. Beſides
all theſe reſolves, they publiſhed daily ſtatements of
the health of the city, to allay the fears of their fellow citizens.

On the 14th of November, the committee reſolved,
that paſſengers coming from Philadelphia to New-
York, might be admitted, in future, together with
their wearing apparel, without reſtriction, as to time,
until further orders from the committee.

The 20th, they declared that they were happy to
announce to their fellow citizens, that health was re-

stored to Philadelphia; but that real danger was still to be apprehended from the bedding and clothing of those who had been ill of the malignant fever; and that they had received satisfactory information, that attempts had been made to ship on freight considerable quantities of beds and bedding from Philadelphia for their city. They therefore resolved that it was inexpedient, to admit the introduction of beds or bedding of any kind, or feathers in bags, or otherwise; also, second-hand wearing apparel of every species, coming from places infected with the yellow fever; and that whosoever should attempt so high-handed an offence as to bring them in, and endanger the lives and health of the inhabitants, would justly merit their resentment and indignation.

The inhabitants of Trenton and Lamberton associated on the 13th of September, and on the 17th passed several resolutions to guard themselves against the contagion. They resolved that a total stop should be put to the landing of all persons from Philadelphia, at any ferry or place from Lamberton to Howell's ferry, four miles above Trenton; that the intercourse by water should be prohibited between Lamberton, or the head of tide water, and Philadelphia; and that all boats from Philadelphia, should be prevented from landing either goods or passengers any where between Bordentown and the head of tide water, that no person whatever should be permitted to come from Philadelphia, or Kensington, while the fever continued; that all persons who should go from within the limits of the association, to either of those places, should be prevented from returning during the continuance of the fever; and finally, that their standing committee should inquire whether any persons, not inhabitants, who had lately come from places infected, and were therefore likely to be infected themselves, were within the limits of the association, and if so, that they should be obliged instantly to leave the said limits.

The 12th of September, the governor of Maryland published a proclamation, subjecting all vessels from Philadelphia to the performance of a quarantine, not exceeding forty days, or as much lefs as might be judged fafe by the health officers. It further ordered, that all perfons going to Baltimore, to Havre de Grace, to the head of Elk, or, by any other route, making their way into that ftate from Philadelphia, or any other place known to be infected with the malignant fever, fhould be fubject to be examined, and prevented from proceeding, by perfons to be appointed for that purpofe, and who were to take the advice and opinion of the medical faculty in every cafe, in order that private affairs and purfuits might not be unneceffarily impeded. This proclamation appointed two health officers for Baltimore.

The people of Baltimore met the 13th of September, and refolved that none of their citizens fhould receive into their houfes any perfons coming from Philadelphia, or other infected place, without producing a certificate from the health officer, or officer of patrole; and that any perfon who violated that refolve, fhould be held up to the public view, as a proper object for the refentment of the town. The 14th, a party of militia was difpatched to take the poffeffion of a pafs on the Philadelphia road, about two miles from Baltimore, to prevent the entrance of any paffengers from Philadelphia without licenfe. Dr. Worthington, the health officer ftationed at this pafs, was directed to refufe permiffion to perfons afflicted with any malignant complaint, or who had not been abfent from Philadelphia, or other infected place, at leaft feven days. The weftern fhore line of Philadelphia ftages was ftopped about the 18th or 19th.

The 30th, the committee of health refolved that no inhabitant of Baltimore, who fhould vifit perfons from Philadelphia, while performing quarantine, fhould be permitted to enter the town, until the time of quarantine was expired, and until it was certainly known that the perfons he had vifited were free from the infection; and that thenceforward no goods capable of conveying infection, that had been landed or packed up in Philadelphia, or other infected place, fhould be permitted to enter the town—nor fhould

any baggage of travellers be admitted, until it had
been expofed to the open air fuch length of time as
the health officer might direct.

CHAP. XI. *Proceedings at Havre de Grace—At Ha-
gerftown.—At Alexandria—At Winchefter.—At Bofton
—At Newbu'yport—In Rhode Ifland—At Newbern—
At Charlefton—In Georgia.—Fafting and prayer.*

THE 25th of September, the inhabitants of Havre
de Grace refolved that no perfon fhould be allowed to crofs the Sufquehannah river at that town, who
did not bring a certificate of his not having lately
come from Philadelphia, or any other infected place ;
and that the citizens of Havre would embody themfelves to prevent any one from croffing without fuch a
certificate.

At Hagerftown, on the 3d of October, it was refolved, that no citizen fhould receive into his houfe
any perfon coming from Philadelphia, fuppofed to
be infected with the malignant fever, until he or fhe
produced a certificate from a health officer; that fhould
any citizen contravene the above refolution, he fhould
be profcribed from all fociety with his fellow citizens ;
that the clothing fent to the troops then in that town,
fhould not be received there, nor fuffered to come
within feven miles thereof; that if any perfon from
Philadelphia, or other infected place, fhould arrive
there, he fhould be required inftantly to depart, and
in cafe of refufal or neglect, be compelled to go without delay; that no merchant, or other perfon, fhould
be fuffered to bring into the town, or open therein,
any goods brought from Philadelphia, or other infected place, until permitted by their committee; and
that the citizens of the town, and its vicinity, fhould
enrol themfelves as a guard, and patrole fuch roads
and paffes as the committee fhould direct.

The governor of Virginia, on the 17th of September, iffued a proclamation, ordering all veffels from
Philadelphia, the Grenades, and the ifland of Tobago,
to perform a quarantine of twenty days, at the an-

chorage ground, off Craney ifland, near the mouth of Elizabeth river.

The corporation of Alexandria ftationed a look-out boat, to prevent all veffels bound to that port, from approaching nearer than one mile, until after examination by the health officer.

The people of Winchefter placed guards at every avenue of the town leading from the Patowmac to ftop all fufpected perfons, packages, &c. coming from Philadelphia, till the health officers fhould infpect them, and either forbid or allow them to pafs.

The legiflature of Maffachufetts were in feffion, at the time the alarm fpread; and they accordingly paffed an exprefs act for guarding againft the impending danger. This act authorifed the felectmen in the different towns to ftop and examine any perfons, baggage, merchandize, or effects, coming or fuppofed to be coming into the towns refpectively, from Philadelphia, or other place infected, or fuppofed to be infected; and fhould it appear to them, or to any officers whom they fhould appoint, that any danger of infection was to be apprehended from fuch perfons, effects, baggage, or merchandize, they were empowered to detain or remove the fame to fuch places as they might fee proper, in order that they might be purified from infection; or to place any perfons fo coming, in fuch places, and under fuch regulations as they might judge neceffary for the public fafety. In purfuance of this act, the governor iffued a proclamation to carry it into effect, the 21ft of September.

The felectmen of Bofton, on the 24th, publifhed their regulations of quarantine, which ordered, that on the arrival of any veffel from Philadelphia, fhe fhould be detained at, or near Rainsford's Ifland, to perform a quarantine not exceeding thirty days, during which time fhe fhould be cleanfed with vinegar, and the explofion of gunpowder between the decks and in the cabin, even though there were no fick perfons on board; that in cafe there were, they fhould be removed to an hofpital, where they fhould be detained till they recovered or were long enough

to afcertain that they had not the infection; that
every veffel, performing quarantine, fhould be depriv-
ed of its boat, and no boat fuffered to approach it,
but by fpecial permiffion; that if any perfon fhould
efcape from veffels performing quarantine, he fhould
be inftantly advertifed, in order that he might be ap·
prehended; that any perfons coming by land from
Philadelphia, fhould not be allowed to enter Bofton,
until twenty one days after their arrival, and their
effects, baggage, and merchandize fhould be opened,
wafhed with vinegar, and fumigated with repeated
explofions of gunpowder. In the conclufion, the felectmen called upon the inhabitants " to ufe their utmoft
vigilance and activity to bring to condign punifhment,
any perfon who fhould be fo daring, and loft to every
idea of humanity, as to come into the town from any
place fuppofed to be infected, thereby endangering
the lives of his fellow men."

The 23d of September, the felectmen of Newbury-
port notified the pilots 'not to bring any veffels from
Philadelphia, higher up Merrimack river, than the
black rocks, until they fhould be examined by the
health officer, and a certificate be obtained from him,
of their being free from infection.

The governor of Rhode Ifland, the 21ft of September, iffued a proclamation, directing the town
councils and other officers, to ufe their utmoft vigilance to caufe the law to prevent the fpreading of contagious diforders to be moft ftrictly executed, more efpecially with refpect to all veffels which fhould arrive
in that ftate, from the Weft Indies, Philadelphia, and
New-York; the extenfion to the latter place was owing to the danger apprehended from the intercourfe
between it and Philadelphia.

The 28th of September, the governor of North
Carolina publifhed his proclamation; requiring the
commiffioners of navigation in the different ports
of the faid ftate, to appoint certain places, where a'l
veffels from the port of Philadelphia, or any other
place in which the malignant fever might prevail,

should perform quarantine for such number of days as they might think proper.

The commissioners of Newbern, on the 30th of September, ordered that until full liberty should be given, vessels arriving from Philadelphia, or any other place in which an infectious disorder might be, should, under a penalty of five hundred pounds, stop and come to anchor at least one mile below the town, and there perform a quarantine for at least ten days; unless their captains should produce from inspectors appointed for the purpose, a certificate that in their opinion the vessels might, with safety to the inhabitants, proceed to the town or harbour, and there land their passengers or cargo. The 18th of October, they ordered, that if any free man should go on board any vessel from Philadelphia, &c. or should bring from on board such vessel, any goods or merchandize, before she was permitted to land her cargo or passengers, he should, for every offence, forfeit five pounds; and if any slave should offend as above, he should be liable to be whipped not exceeding fifty lashes, and his master to pay five pounds.

The governor of S. Carolina, published a proclamation, subjecting Philadelphia vessels to quarantine, the date of which I cannot ascertain. The inhabitants of Charleston, on the 8th of October, had a meeting, at which they resolved, that no vessel from the river Delaware, either directly or after having touched at any other port of the United States, should be permitted to pass Charleston bar, till the citizens had again assembled, and declared themselves satisfied that the disorder had ceased in Philadelphia. If any vessel, contrary thereto, should cross the bar, the governor should be requested to compel it to quit the port, and return to sea.

The governor of Georgia, on the 4th of October, published a proclamation, ordering all vessels from Philadelphia, which should arrive in Savannah river, to remain in Tybee creek, or in other parts like distant from the town, until the health officer of the port should, on examination, certify, that no malignant or cert   disease was on board. All persons contravening this proclamation, were to be profecuted, and fubjected to the pains and penalties by law pointed out.

The people of Augufta, in that ftate, were as active and vigilant as their northern neighbours, to guard againft the threatening danger.

The inhabitants of Reading, in Pennfylvania, had a meeting the 24th of September, and paffed fundry refolutions, viz. that no dry goods fhould be imported into that borough from Philadelphia, or any other place infected with a malignant fever, until the expiration of one month from that date, unlefs permiffion was had from the inhabitants convened at a town-meeting; that no perfon from Philadelphia, or any other infected place, fhould be allowed to enter, until they fhould have undergone the examination of a phyfician, and obtained his opinion of their being free from infection; that no ftage-waggon fhould be permitted to bring paffengers from Philadelphia, or other place infected, into the borough; and that all communication, by ftages, fhould be difcontinued for one month, unlefs fooner permitted by the inhabitants.

At Bethlehem, a meeting was held on the 26th of September; at which it was refolved, that perfons from Philadelphia, fhould perform a quarantine of twelve days, before their entrance into the town. A fimilar refolve was foon after entered into at Nazareth. But at neither place was it obferved with any ftrictnefs. No guard was appointed. And the affertion of any decent traveller, apparently in health, with refpect to the time of his abfence from Philadelphia, was confidered as fufficient to be relied on, without reforting to formal proof.

Various precautions were obferved in other places; but I am not able to give a ftatement of them, not having procured an account of their refolves or proceedings.

The calamity of Philadelphia, while it roufed the circumfpection of the timid in various places, excited the pious to offer up their prayers to Almighty God for our relief, comfort, and fupport. Various days were appointed for humiliation, fafting, and prayer,

H

for this purpofe. In New York, the 20th of September; in Bofton, September 26th; in Albany, the ift of October; in Baltimore the 3d; in Richmond, the 9th; in Providence, the fame day; the fynod of Philadelphia fixed on the 24th of October; the proteftant epifcopal churches in Virginia, November 6; the Dutch fynod of New York, November 13; the fynod of New York and New Jerfey, November 20. At Hartford, daily prayers were offered up for our relief for fome time.

CHAP. XII. *Conflict between the law of felf-prefervation and the law of charity. The law of charity victorious.*

WHILE our citizens were profcribed in feveral cities and towns—hunted up like felons in fome—debarred admittance and turned back in others, whether found or infected—it is with extreme fatisfaction I have to record a conduct totally different, which cannot fail to make an indelible impreffion on the minds of the people of Philadelphia, and call forth the moft lively emotions of gratitude.

At Woodbury, in New Jerfey, at an early period of the diforder, a meeting was held for the purpofe of determining on what fteps were requifite to be taken. A motion was made to ftop all intercourfe with Philadelphia. But, four perfons only having rifen to fupport it, it dropped, and our citizens were allowed free entrance.

A refpectable number of the inhabitants of Springfield, in New Jerfey, met the firft day of October, and after a full confideration of the diftreffes of our citizens, paffed a refolve, offering their town as an afylum to the people flying from Philadelphia, and directing their committee to provide a fuitable place as an hofpital for the fick. The rev. Jacob V. Artfdalen, Matthias Meeker, and Matthias Denman, took the lead in this honourable bufinefs.

I have been informed, by a perfon of credit, that the inhabitants of Elizabeth town have purfued the fame liberal plan, as thofe of Springfield; but have not

been able to procure a copy of their refolves or proceedings on the fubject.

At Cheftertown in Maryland; a place was appointed, at a diftance from the town, for the reception of
fuch travellers and others, as might have the diforder. It was provided with every neceffary—and a
phyfician engaged to attend the fick.

An afylum has likewife been offered to Philadelphians, by feveral of the inhabitants of Elkton, in Maryland ; and the offer was couched in terms of the
utmoft fympathy for our fufferings. A place on the
fame plan as that at Chefter, was fitted up near the
town.

At Eafton, in Pennfylvania, the only precaution obferved, was to direct the emigrants from Philadelphia, to abftain for a week from intercourfe with the
inhabitants.

The people of Wilmington have acted in the moft
friendly manner towards our diftreffed citizens. At
firft they were a little fcared, and refolved on the eftablifhment of a quarantine and guards. But they
immediately dropped thefe precautions, and received
the people from Philadelphia with the moft perfect
freedom. They erected an hofpital for the reception of
our infected citizens, which they fupplied with neceffaries. Yet of eight or ten perfons from Philadelphia,
who died in that town, with the malignant fever,
only one was fent to the hofpital. The others were
nurfed and attended in the houfes where they fell
fick. Humane, tender, and friendly, as were the worthy inhabitants of Wilmington in general, two characters have diftinguifhed themfelves in fuch a very
extraordinary manner, as to deferve particular notice. Thefe are doctor Way, and major Bufh, whofe
houfes were always open to the fugitives from Philadelphia, whom they received without the fmalleft ap-
prehenfion, and treated with a degree of genuine hof-
pitality, that reflects the higheft honour on them. In
the exercife of this virtue, they were not confined by a
narrow regard to their particular friends or acquain-
tance—but entertained, with equal humanity, whole

families of perfons who were utter ftrangers to them. This was of the more importance, and operated as a heavier tax on them, as, I believe, there was only one tavern-keeper, Brinton, whofe houfe was open for people from Philadelphia: and it was confequently fo crouded in general, as frequently to render it difficult to procure admittance.

The inftances of this kind, through this extenfive country, have been very few; but they are therefore only the more precious, and ought to be held up to public approbation. May they operate on people, at a future day, in fimilar cafes of dreadful calamity, and teach them to temper their caution with as much humanity and tendernefs to the diftreffed fugitives, as prudence will allow—and not involve, in one indifcriminate profcription, the healthy and infected.

CHAP. XIII. *Diforder fatal to the doctors—to the clergy—to drunkards—to filles de joie—to maid fervants—to the poor—and in clofe ftreets.—Lefs deftructive to the French—and to the negroes.*

RARELY has it happened, that fo large a proportion of the gentlemen of the faculty have funk beneath the labours of their very dangerous profeffion, as on this occafion. In five or fix weeks, exclufive of medical ftudents, no lefs than ten phyficians have been fwept off, doctors Hutchinfon, Morris, Linn, Pennington, Dodds, Johnfon, Glentworth, Phile, Graham and Green. Scarcely one of the practifing doctors that remained in the city, efcaped ficknefs. Some were three, four, and five times confined.

To the clergy it has likewife proved very fatal. Expofed, in the exercife of the laft duties to the dying, to equal danger with the phyficians, it is not furprifing that fo many of them have fallen. Their names are, the rev. Alexander Murray, of the proteftant epifcopal church—the rev. F. A. Fleming and the rev. Laurence Graefsl of the Roman catholic—the rev. John Winkhaufe, of the German reformed—the rev. James Sproat, of the prefbyterian—the rev. Wil-, liam Dougherty, of the methodift church—and like-wife four noted preachers of the Friends fociety, Daniel Offley, Hufon Langftroth, Michael Minier; and, Charles Williams. Seven clergymen have been in the greateft danger from this diforder, the rev. R. Blackwell, rev. Jofeph Pilmore. rev. William Rogers, rev. Chriftopher V. Keating, rev. Frederic Schmidt, the rev. Jofeph Turner, and the rev. Robert Annan ; but they have all recovered.

Among the women, the mortality has not, by any means, been fo great, as among the men,* nor among the old and infirm as among the middle-aged and robuft.

To tipplers and drunkards, and to men who lived high, and were of a corpulent habit of body, this diforder was very fatal. Of thefe, many were feized, and the recoveries were very rare.

To the *filles de joie*, it has been equally fatal. The wretched, debilitated ftate of their conftitutions, rendered them an eafy prey to this dreadful diforder, which very foon terminated their miferable career.

To hired fervant maids it has been very deftructive. Numbers of them fled away—of thofe who remained, very many fell, who had behaved with an extraordinary degree of fidelity.

It has been dreadfully deftructive among the poor. It is very probable, that at leaft feven-eighths of the number of the dead, were of that clafs. The inhabitants of dirty houfes have feverely expiated their neglect of cleanlinefs and decency, by the numbers of them that have fallen facrifices. Whole families, in fuch houfes, have funk into one filent, undiftinguifhing grave.

The mortality in confined ftreets, fmall allies, and clofe houfes, debarred of a free circulation of air, has exceeded, in a great proportion, that in the large ftreets and well-aired houfes. In fome of the allies, a third

* In many congregations, the deaths of men have been nearly twice as numerous as thofe of women.

or fourth of the whole of the inhabitants are no more. In 30 houses, the whole number in Pewter Platter alley, 32 people died: and in a part of Market-street, containing 170 houses, only 39. The streets in the suburbs, that had the benefit of the country air, especially towards the west part of the city, have suffered little. Of the wide, airy streets, none lost so many people as Arch, near Water-street, which may be accounted for, by its proximity to the original seat of the disorder. It is to be particularly remarked, that in general, the more remote the streets were from Water street, the less of the calamity they experienced.

From the effects of this disorder, the French newly settled in Philadelphia, have been in a very remarkable degree exempt†. To what this may be owing, is a subject deserving particular investigation*. By some it has been ascribed to their despising the danger. But, though this may have had some effect, it will not certainly account for it altogether ; as it is well known that many of the most courageous persons in Philadelphia, have been among its victims. By many of the French, the great fatality of the disorder has been attributed to the vast quantities of crude and unwholesome fruits brought to our markets, and consumed by all classes of people.

When the yellow fever prevailed in South Carolina, the negroes, according to that accurate observer, dr. Lining, were wholly free from it. " There is " something very singular in the constitution of the " negroes," says he, " which renders them not liable " to this fever ; for though many of them were as " much exposed as the nurses to this infection, yet I " never knew one instance of this fever among them, " though they are equally subject with the white peo-

---

† The French who had been long established here, were nearly as much affected as the natives.

* The frequent use the French make of *lavements*, at all times, may probably account for their escaping so very generally as they did. These purify the bowels, help to discharge the foul matter, and remove costiveness, which is one of the most certain supports of this and other disorders.

.'' ple.to the bilious fever*.'' The fame idea prevailed for a confiderable time, in Philadelphia; but it was erroneous. They did not efcape the diforder; however, there were fcarcely any of them feized at firft, and the number that were finally affected, was not great; and, as I am informed by an eminent doctor, '' it '' yielded to the power of medicine in them more ea- '' fily than in the whites.'' The error that prevailed on this fubject had a very falutary effect; for, at an early period of the diforder, hardly any white nurfes could be procured; and, had the negroes been equally terrified, the fufferings of the fick, great as they actually were, would have been exceedingly aggravated, At the period alluded to, the elders of the African church met, and offered their affiftance to the mayor, to procure nurfes for the fick, and aid in burying the dead. Their offers were accepted; and Abfalom Jones, Richard Allen, and William Gray, undertook the management of thefe two-feveral fervices. The great demand for nurfes, afforded an opportunity for impofition, which was eagerly feized by fome of the vileft of the blacks†. They extorted two, three, four, and even five dollars a night for fuch attendance, as would have been well paid by a fingle dollar. Some of them were even detected in plundering the houfes of the fick. But it is unjuft to caft a cenfure on the whole, for this fort of conduct, as many people have done. The fervices of Jones, Allen, and Gray, and others of their colour, have been very great, and demand public gratitude.

On examining the books of the hofpital at Bufhhill, it appears, that there were nearly twenty blacks received there, of whom about three-fourths died.

* Effays and obfervations, vol. II. page 407.
† The extortion here mentioned, was very far from being confined to the negroes: many of the white nurfes behaved with equal rapacity.

C H A P. XIV. *State of the weather. Attempt to refute the opinion that cold and rain extinguished the diforder. Average-table of mortality.*

THE weather, during the whole of the months of August and September, and moft part of October, was remarkably dry and fultry. Rain appeared as if entirely at an end. Various indications, which in fcarcely any former inftance had failed to produce wet weather, difappointed the expectations, the wifhes, and the prayers of the citizens. The diforder raged with increafed violence as the feafon advanced towards the fall months. The mortality was much greater in September, than in Auguft—and ftill greater in the beginning and till the middle of October, than in September. It very particularly merits attention, that though nearly all the hopes of the inhabitants refted on cold and rain, efpecially the latter, yet the diforder died away with hardly any rain, and a very moderate degree of cold. Its virulence may be faid to have expired on the 23d, 24th, 25th, and 26th of October. The fucceeding deaths were, moftly, of thofe long fick. Few perfons took the diforder afterwards. Thofe days were nearly as warm as many of the moft fatal ones; in the middle ftage of the complaint, the thermometer being at 60, 59, 71, and 72. To account for this fatiffactorily, is above our feeble powers. In fact, the whole of the diforder, from its firft appearance to its final clofe, has fet human wifdom and calculation at defiance.

The idea held up in the preceding paragraph, has been controverted by many ; and, as the extinction of malignant diforders, generated in fummer or the early part of fall, has been univerfally afcribed to the fevere cold and heavy rains of the clofe of the fall, or the winter, it is afferted that ours muft have fhared the fame fate. It therefore becomes necef-fary to ftate the reafons for the contrary opinion.

The extinction of thefe diforders, according to the generally-received idea on this fubject, arifes from cold,

or rain, or both together. If from the former, how
shall we account for a greater mortality in September,
than in August, whereas the degree of heat was considerably abated? How shall we account for a greater
mortality in the first part of October than in September, although the heat was still abating? If rain
be the efficient cause of arresting the disorder, as is
supposed by those who attribute its declension to the
rain on the evening of the 15th* of October, how
shall we account for the inefficacy of a constant rain
during the whole terrible twelfth of October, when
one hundred and eleven souls were summoned out of
this world, and a hundred and four the day following? To make the matter more plain, I request the
reader's attention to the following statement :—

		Thermom. at 3 P. M.	Deaths.	Wind.	Weather.
Sept.	19	70	61	SW	fair.
	20	69	67	SE	hazy.
	21	78	57		fair.
	22	83	76		fair.
Oct.	10	74	93	NW	fair.
	11	74	119	W	fair.
	12	64	111	NW	rain.
	13	69	104	NW	fair.
	23	60	54	W	fair.
	24	59	38	NW	fair.
	25	71	35	S	fair, high wind.
	26	72	23	SW	cloudy.

An examination of this table, by any man unbiaf-
sed by the received opinion, will, I think, convince
him of the justice of the hypothesis which I have advanced—that the increase or abatement of the violence of the disorder, depended on other causes than
the degrees of heat, cold, rainy or dry weather. Here
is the most palpable proof. The average of the thermometer, the four first quoted days, was 75 °—the average of the deaths 65.5. The second four days, the
thermometer averaged 70.25, although the frightful
average of deaths was, 106.75. And on the last four

* The rain on this evening was not by any means so great
as that o

days, the thermometer averaged 65.5, whereas the deaths were only 37.5. To facilitate the comparifon, I fubjoin an abftract of the preceding ftatement.

	therm.	deaths.
Average of Sept. 19, 20, 21, and 22,	75	65
of Oct. 10, 11, 12, and 13,	70.25	106.75
of Oct. 23, 24, 25, and 26,	65.5	37.5

Thus, thofe days on which the mortality was at its higheft ftage, were five degrees colder than thofe when the deaths had been only five eighths. And the difference of five degrees between the fecond and the third four days, will not be pretended to account for a decreafe of very nearly two thirds. To try the fyftem of heat, cold, and rain, ftill further, let us examine the four laft days of Auguft. On thofe days the thermometer averaged 79.5.; yet the deaths were only 20.75.

I here annex the weekly average of the thermometer and of the deaths, from the firft of Auguft to the 7th of November, for the reader's infpection[*].

	Average of thermometer.	Average of deaths.
Auguft 1 to 7,	84	9
8 to 14,	85	7
15 to 21,	83	7
22 to 28,	77	15
92 to 31,	85	17
Sept. 1 to 7,	81	19
8 to 14,	74	35
15 to 21,	75	65
22 to 28,	76	70
29 and 30,	74	60
Oct. 1 to 7,	71	72
8 to 14,	71	100
15 to 21,	58	67
22 to 28,	58	39
29 to 31,	46	18
Nov. 1 to 7,	58	15

From the above table it appears, that during the

---

[*] When the fractions exceed half, an unit is added; when they are below half, they are rejected.

month of September, there was a rapid increase regularly of deaths, except on the 29th and 30th, although the weather was growing cooler nearly the whole time. Let any advocate of the theory of cold and rain, compare the first week in September with the second week in October. He will see that the former was ten degrees warmer than the latter, yet the mortality of the one, was only a fifth part of the other. If he will, after this, say that the difference of 13 degrees between the second week in October and the 3d and 4th, will account for a reduction of the mortality from 100 to 67, and then to 39, I can only answer, that an inveterate prejudice too often clouds the reason, and renders it impossible to see the truth, however evident.

In opposition to what I have advanced, it has been observed, that the unfavourable effects of very sultry days were felt for several succeeding ones. This is a weak resource, as will appear from examining the table. The heat of the first and second weeks in October was the same: yet the mortality in the second was nearly one half more than in the first. The heat of the fourth was equal to that of the third, although in the former the deaths were nearly double what they were in the latter.

I hope, therefore, the reader will acknowledge, that the Great Disposer of winds and rains, took his own time, and without the means, either moral or physical, on which we placed our chief reliance, to rescue the remnant of us from destruction.

CHAP. XV.—*Origin of the disorder.*

THIS disorder has most unquestionably been imported from the West Indies. As yet, however, owing to various obvious reasons, it is difficult to fix, with absolute precision, on the vessel or vessels, (for it is very probable it came in several, from the different infected islands) by which it was introduced. That it is an imported disorder, rests on the following reasons, each of which, singly, justifies the theory, but all, collectively, eſtabliſh it to the ſatisfaction of every candid and reaſonable man.

1ſt. The yellow fever exiſted in ſeveral of the Weſt India iſlands a long time before its appearance here*.

2d. Various veſſels from thoſe iſlands arrived here in July.

3d. Scarcely any precautions were uſed to guard a-gainſt the diſorder.

4th. A reſpectable citizen of Philadelphia, ſuper-cargo of one of our veſſels, ſaw, in July, ſix or ſeven people ſick of this fever on board a brig at Cape François bound for our port†.

5th. A veſſel from Cape François, which arrived here in July, loſt ſeveral of her people with this fever, on her paſſage.

---

* *Extract from a London paper, of Auguſt* 13, 1793.

" The plague, brought from Bulam, which firſt made its
" appearance at Grenada, has ſpread moſt alarmingly. Eighty
" perſons died in one day, at Grenada of this epidemic. The
" hurricane months juſt coming on, are not likely to make it
" leſs violent in its effects."
" [It appears by a ſubſequent paragraph in the ſame paper,
" that the diſeaſe was aſcertained to be the yellow fever.]"

Extract from the Courier, a London paper, of Auguſt 24.

" Before the fleet left Antigua ſo great was the apprehenſion
" entertained there of the plague, that all veſſels from Grena-
" da, were obliged to perform quarantine, and all letters from
" the latter iſland, were ſmoaked at the former. The infection
" was reported to have reached Dominica "

Extract from the Obſerver, a London paper, of Auguſt 25.

" The plague, we are diſtreſſed to hear, has made its appear-
" ance in ſeveral of our Weſt India iſlands At Grenada, and
" Dominica, the ſymptoms are ſaid to be highly alarming."

Extract from a Kingſton paper, of October 12.

" The iſlands of Barbadoes and Dominica continue to be
" afflicted with a malignant fever, about 300 white inhabitants
" have periſhed in the former, and near 500 in the latter."

† To any enquirer I am ready to communicate the name of the ſupercargo, and the name of the brig.

6th. A perfon from Cape François, died of this fever at Marcus Hook‡—and another at Chefter§.

7th. The veffels in which thofe perfons arrived, and which were infected with the effluvia of the fick and dead, came freely to our wharves, and particularly to that very one where the diforder made its firft appearance.

8th. Perfons fick of the yellow fever have been landed in our city from veffels arrived from the Weft Indies*.

9th. Dead bodies have been feen depofited fecretly on board fome of thofe veffels.

10th. There is the ftrongeft reafon to believe, that the beds and bedding of the fick and dead were not deftroyed, but, on the contrary, brought into our city.

11th. This diforder had every characteriftic fymptom that marked it on former occafions, when its importation was unqueftioned.

Laftly, Of all the reafons advanced to fupport the opinion of its having been generated here, the only one, that has even the appearance of plaufibility, viz. the influence of a tropical feafon, fuch as we had laft fummer, is unanfwerably refuted by the concurring teftimony of Lind, Lining, Warren, and Bruce, who, in the moft unequivocal manner, have declared that it does not depend on the weather.

" It does not appear, from the moft accurate ob-
" fervations of the variations of the weather, or any
" difference of the feafons, which I have been able to
" make for feveral years paft, that this fever is *any*
" *way caufed*, or much influenced by them; for I
" have feen it *at all times*, and in *all feafons*, in the

---

‡ I do hereby declare, that I was at Marcus Hook late in July, when a woman, who had been landed there from one of the veffels lately from Cape Francois, died. that I was informed by a French perfon, a neighbour, that fhe died of the yellow fever, that this perfon burned a quantity of tar at the door, for the purpofe, as he informed me, of purifying the air.
                                               JOHN MASSEY.

§ My information of the death of this perfon is derived from a letter written by dr. William Martin to dr. Currie.

* Major Hodgdon and others can teftify to the truth of this.

" coolest, as well as in the hottest time of the
" year."*

" This fever does not seem to take its origin from
" any particular constitution of the weather, indepen-
" dent of infectious miasmata, as dr. Warren has for-
" merly well observed; for within these twenty-five
" years, it has been only four times epidemical in
" this town, namely in the autumns of the years
" 1732, 39, 45, and 48, though none of those years,
" (excepting that of 1739, whose summer and au-
" tumn were remarkably rainy) were either warm-
" er or more rainy, (and some of them less so) than
" the summers and autumns were in several other
" years, in which we had not one instance of any
" one seized with this fever : which is contrary to
" what would have happened, if particular constitutions
" of the weather, were productive of it, without infecti-
" ous miasmata†."

" In omni anni tempestate, sese effert hic morbus;
" symptomata autem graviora observantur, ubi calor
" magnus cum multa humiditate conjungitur‡."

C H A P. XVI. Desultory facts and reflexions. A collection of scraps§.

THE want of a lazaretto, whither persons labouring under contagious disorders, might be sent;
and of a proper law on the subject, empowering the
civil authority to interpose with the necessary energy,

---

* Hillary on diseases of Barbadoes, page 146.
† Lining, Essays and observations, political and literary, vol.
II page 406.
‡ Bruce, quoted by Lind on hot climates, 237.
§ This and the succeeding chapter calls for some apology.
Many of the anecdotes herein related, are of little importance,
except from their having a tendency to reflect light on the state
of the public mind during a time in which men were most completely taken by surprise. Considering the subject in this point
of view, hardly any occurrence, of so eventful a period, ought
to be suffered to sink in oblivion. Some, of a ludicrous turn, are
introduced as a relief to the sombre complexion of a narrative,
in which the predominant characters are death and destruction,
and a cold regard for self alone.

at the firft inroad of fuch a dreadful deftroyer, has
been the caufe of our late fufferings ; for, humanly
fpeaking, had decifive meafures been adopted any
time before the firft of September, while the diforder
exifted only in one ftreet, and in a few houfes in that
ftreet, there can be little doubt, that it might have
been very foon extinguifhed. But the former fufferings of this place in 1762, were foon forgotten—
and no fteps taken to provide for the removal of
fuch an evil in future, after it fhould invade the city.
It is to be hoped our legiflature, as well as that of
every ftate in the union, will fee the propriety of giving this important fubject the confideration it fo amply deferves, and of making provifion againft like
calamities in future. In Italy, at Spalato, where the
plague raged fifteen or twenty years ago, if the infected did not reveal their fituation to the proper authority, they were fubjected to capital punifhment ;
and the fame penalty was denounced againft fuch as
did not inform of infected perfons, when they knew
of them. This is too fevere for the paternal mild-
nefs of our criminal code ; but fome penalties ought
to be denounced in fuch cafes. Indeed, were lazaret-
tos on a proper eftablifhment, it would be an object
of defire with the fick, to be tranfported to them.

—◦◦◦—

It is hardly conceivable that the funeral of entire
ftrangers could afford fubject of fatisfaction. Yet they
have produced that effect. After being fo long accuftomed to behold the bodies of the dead, drawn to the
grave on the fhafts of a chair, the fight of a corpfe
carried by men to be interred, afforded fomething like
the appearance of former times ; and I believe the
fatisfaction excited by that confideration abforbed
every thought of the deceafed.

—◦◦◦—

The appearance of moft of the grave yards in Philadelphia is extremely awful. They exhibit a ftrong like-
nefs of ploughed fields ; and were any thing capable

of ftamping on our breafts indelible impreffions of the uncertainty of the tenure by which we hold our very precarious exiftence, a turn though one of our burial grounds could not poffibly fail to produce that effect. But it is to be feared, that with the danger will vanifh all recollection of the diftreffing fcenes we have paffed through.

— ⊛ ⊛ ⊛ —

It has been denied that a perfon is twice fufceptible of the yellow fever. The opinion, as it has a good tendency, to infpire confidence in convalefcents, and in thofe who have quite recovered, might perhaps as well be fuffered to pafs uncontroverted, were not truth the object. Several perfons in this city, have been twice fick with this diforder. I know it is ufual to call this a relapfe. But relapfe or not, thofe people whom I mean, have been ill—have recovered entirely—and been a second time taken down. Some of them are now no more, witnefs mr. Fleming. Mr. William Young was worfe the fecond time than the firft.

— ⊛ ⊛ ⊛ —

One obfervation, of great importance to the caufe of humanity, efcaped me in the former editions, and ought to be very particularly attended to in every fuch dreadful crifis as we have experienced. Of the very large number of perfons who have fallen under this diforder, it is not improbable that a half or a third have perifhed merely for want of neceffary care and attention, owing to the extraordinary panic. Almoft all the remarkable cafes of recovery are to be afcribed, under providence, to the fidelity of hufbands, wives, children, and fervants, who braved the danger, and determined to obey the dictates of humanity. There are various inftances, of perfons who may be faid to have been by thefe means fnatched from the grafp of death; having been fo far reduced, as to have their coffins made.——And for the encouragement of thofe who may, at any other time, or in any other place, have friends or relatives in this diforder, let it be remarked, that few of those who discharged their duty to their families, have suffered by it. There are instances of individuals, who have nursed and attended on six, eight and ten persons unremittingly, in their own houses, without ever taking the infection. Others, before their own illness, and after their recovery, nursed and restored their families. William Young had no less than ten in his house sick, and nearly all at one time. He attended on them till he was taken ill; and, during his sickness, gave directions for the management of them, as effectually as if he was well. After his recovery, he again attended them himself. Of his whole family, his wife only died; and it is supposed her death was accelerated by her being in an advanced stage of pregnancy. There are cases of single persons having the disorder in large families of eight, ten, and twelve, and none catching it from them. In the family of David Clarke, who died of the malignant fever, there were no less than twenty-two persons, not one of whom caught the infection, altho' he had the same attention paid him by all his family, as if he had been in any other disorder. Not one of the carters employed by the committee in the very dangerous office of removing the sick and burying the dead, ever had it*. The nurses at Bush-hill have all escaped, except two; as have the worthy managers. Thomas Boyles, the tenant, who occupied the building at Bushhill, at the time it was taken as an hospital, that is, the 31st of August, lived there until

---

* Let not the humble sphere of life in which he moves, prevent me from here mentioning a worthy and faithful man, Thomas Wilkinson, employed by the committee, in burying the dead, and removing the sick, from their organization till the extinction of the disorder. Such was the noxious situation of many dead bodies, that he frequently returned vomiting from the performance of his duty. In one instance, in raising the corpse of a woman several days dead, he was covered with putrescent blood. Yet he still persevered in the most unwearied manner, through dangers, that render his preservation equally astonishing with that of Girard, Helm, Helmuth, mrs. Saville, and others. It is to be hoped the corporation will find some comfortable situation for him, in which to pass the remainder of his days.

K

the 29th of October, with his wife and six children, none of whom were ever affected with the malignant fever. Let these instances suffice at all future times to prevent fear from totally overpowering the understanding, and producing scenes of cruelty that make a feeling being blush for his species.

—◆◆◆—

Among the country people, large quantities of wild pigeons in the spring are regarded as certain indications of an unhealthy summer. Whether or not this prognostic has ever been verified before, I cannot tell. But it is very certain, that during the last spring, the numbers of those birds brought to market, were immense. Never, perhaps, were there so many before.

—◆◆◆—

Several classes of people were highly benefited by the public distress. Coffin-makers had full employment, and in general high prices for their work. Most of the retail stores being shut up, those that remained open, had an uncommon demand ; as the whole of the business. was divided among a few. Those who had carriages to hire, to transport families to the country, received whatever they pleased to require. The holders of houses at from three, to twenty miles from the city, who chose to rent the whole or part of them, had high rents. The two notaries, who protested for the banks, profited highly by the absence of the merchants and traders.

—◆◆◆—

I have learned with great pleasure, that a few landlords, commiserating the distresses of their tenants, have come to the very humane resolution of remitting the payment of rents due during the prevalence of the disorder. Were they to enter into resolutions generally to do the same, it would reflect honour on them. But there are some, whose hardened hearts know no compassion, and who will have " the pound " of flesh—the penalty of the bond." Indeed, when he disorder was at the highest stage, some landlords feized, the fmall property of poor roomkeepers, who were totally unable to pay their rent. A man wrote to the committee, informing them that the poverty of his tenants rendered it impoffible for them to pay him ; he therefore begged the committee would, as they were appointed to relieve the poor, pay the arrears due him ! Another perfon, a wealthy widow, procured recommendations for fome poor roomkeepers, her tenants ; and the committee gave them each a fmall fum. As foon as they had received it, fhe feized the money and their clothes !

A man loft his wife with the diforder. He had, it himfelf, loft his fight totally, and was left pennylefs, with two infant children. Yet his landlord, before his convalefcence was complete, feized his clothes and furniture, and turned him out of doors ! ! !

> " You may as well ufe queftion with the wolf,
> " Why he hath made the ewe bleat for the lamb,
> " As feek to foften that (than which what's harder ?)
> " His flinty heart."——— SHAKESPEARE.

—◆◆◆—

I hope the reader takes more pleafure in perufing cafes reflecting honour on human nature, than thofe of a different defcription. An amiable woman in New York, feeling for the fituation of the numerous orphans in this city, wrote to a member of the committee, to choofe her one of them, as nearly refembling a child fhe had loft, as poffible. She particularly defired one without connexions, if fuch could be procured. She propofes to adopt it, and, with her hufband, to beftow on it all the tendernefs one of her own would have had. Would it not be unjuft to withhold her name ? Every reader anfwers, yes—and I will therefore reveal it---Sufan Willet. Several applications of a fimilar nature have been made by fome of our own citizens.

—◆◆◆—

In the fummer of 1791, the yellow fever prevailed in New York, in a part of Water-ftreet, and in proportion to the fphere of its action, was as fatal there as it has been here. It began in Auguft, and continued till the middle of September, when it totally difappeared, and has never fince vifited that place. This fhould eafe the fears of many among us, who, always viewing the black fide of every thing, terrify people with their prognoftications, that we fhall have it again next fpring or fummer. All the fymptoms were full as dangerous and alarming in New York, as in Philadelphia. Many perfons died in three days; " ftupor, delirium, " yellownefs, the black vomit, and death, rapidly fuc-" ceeding each other."‡ It fpread no farther at that time, than the one ftreet, although no precautions, as far as I can learn, were taken to prevent its extenfion. The fame fpecies of diforder raged in this city in 1762, with great violence. It difappeared in the month of November, and has not from that time until this year vifited Philadelphia.

The fummer and fall of this year have been unhealthy in many parts of the union, as well as in Philadelphia. At Lynn, in Maffachufetts, I have been informed, but have no means of afcertaining the truth or falfehood of the report, that a malignant fever, not unlike ours, prevailed in Auguft. In many of the towns of Virginia, intermittent fevers have been much more prevalent and mortal than they have been at former periods. Georgetown and its vicinity, which are in general very healthy, loft, in the courfe of a few weeks in fummer, an unexampled number of people by the flux, which diforder has raged with great violence in many parts of America. The influenza has generally fpread through the union, and been very fatal. It has been twice in Vermont, where likewife the putrid fore throat has carried off numbers. At Harrifburg and Middletown, in this ftate, the flux and a putrid fever have been extremely deftructive, and fwept away, I am credibly informed, a fifteenth

‡ Letter from a phyfician in New York, to his friend in New Jerfey. Federal Gazette, Sept. 21, 1793.

part of the inhabitants. Delaware ftate, particularly. Kent county, has fuffered much from fall fevers, which have produced a very great mortality. At Dover, in the fame ftate, a bilious colic raged with great violence, during laft fummer, and was extremely fatal. At Pauling's Kill, in Suffex county, New Jerfey, a bilious and remittent fever has made very great havoc. And various other places have experienced a mortality, very uncommon, and which, but for the calamity of Philadelphia abforbing public attention every where, and being the ftandard of comparifon, would have created great alarms and uneafinefs.

— ✥✥✥ —

Of the number of citizens who fled away, it is difficult to form any accurate eftimate. In the city, from Vine to South ftreet, which has been furveyed by a man employed by the committee, of 21,000 inhabitants, the number of abfent people is ftated to be 8600. But as this bufinefs was feveral weeks performing, confiderable variations muft neceffarily have taken place. The emigration was not finifhed in thofe ftreets examined in the early part of his progrefs,—and towards the latter part, the returns had been already confiderable. One may be fuppofed to balance the other, and the removals in the liberties to have been equal to thofe in the city. We fhall therefore probably not err much, when we eftimate the number who left the city at about 17,000. This is not fo many as I formerly fuppofed, having eftimated them at 23,000. Which of the two is accurate, or whether either of them is fo, I leave the reader to determine.

— ✥✥✥ —

The effect of fear in predifpofing the body for the yellow fever and other diforders, and increafing their malignance, when taken, is well known. The following exception to the general rule, which may be depended on, is curious and interefting. A young woman, whofe fears were fo very prevalent, as not only to render her unhappy from the commencement of the diforder, but even to interfere with the happinefs of the family with whom fhe lived, had to attend on feven perfons, all of whom were in a very dangerous ftate, and one of whom died. Her attendance was affiduous and unremitted for nearly three weeks. Yet fhe has never been in the flighteft degree affected.

—◈◈◈—

The watches and clocks in this city, during the diforder, were almoft always wrong. Hardly any of the watchmakers remained—and few people paid attention how time paffed. One night, the watchmen cried ten o'clock when it was only nine, and continued the miftake all the fucceeding hours.

—◈◈◈—

The Hope, a veffel from Londonderry, arrived in our river towards the end of Auguft. The paffengers had a malignant diforder among them, in confequence of which, orders were iffued to have them landed at State Ifland, that they might undergo examination. Neverthelefs, feveral of them came to the city, and added to the dangers already exifting. The mayor, on the 3d of September, iffued a proclamation, calling upon the citizens not only to ufe their endeavours to detect fuch as had arrived, and to prevent others from coming, without procuring the proper certificates ; but to make report to one of the magiftrates, of the names of thofe by whom they were harboured, that they might be profecuted according to law. On this fubject an obvious reflexion arifes, which I will not fupprefs. Our citizens have generally been in the habit of feverely cenfuring the inhabitants of thofe places in which very ftrict precautions were taken, to prevent the fpreading of the diforder that prevailed here ; and yet we fee that our own conduct, in a cafe nearly fimilar, has not been very different. I would not wifh to be underftood as if I meant to juftify the whole of the proceedings that took place every where ; far from it ; fome of them have been to the laft degree fevere, and unneceffarily fo ; for all the cautions requifite, were compatible with a fmall degree of attention to the comfort and convenience of fellow citizens, in good health, travelling for business, for pleasure, or the preservation of health, and even of life.—Whereas in many places it would appear as if the harshest mode of carrying harsh measures into effect, was purposely adopted. My intention is merely to show, that such as indiscriminately vilify those who have resorted to precautions dictated by prudence, do not weigh the matter in the scales of impartial justice.

— ❧❧❧ —

Governor Moultrie's proclamation, announcing the existence of the malignant fever in the Grenadas, &c. and ordering a quarantine, is dated the 7th of June.

— ❧❧❧ —

Some of the postmasters, in the different states, used the precaution to dip Philadelphia letters into vinegar with a pair of tongs, before they handled them. Several of the subscribers for Philadelphia papers, made their servants sprinkle them with vinegar, and dry them at the fire, before they would venture to touch them.

— ❧❧❧ —

Joseph Inskeep attended several sick persons in a family near him. When he was ill himself, he wanted assistance*, and sent for some of them to attend him— but they ungratefully refused! O Shame! where is thy blush?

— ❧❧❧ —

Many of our citizens, who fled from the city, neglected or forgot to leave their servants money enough for their support; so that some of these poor creatures had to depend for sustenance on the charity of their neighbours.

— ❧❧❧ —

Some of our unemployed tradesmen wished to procure work at the new roads now making. But the

* His wife was ill at the same time.

people who were employed, agreed, that if they were engaged, that they would all abandon their work; so that the overseers were obliged to renounce the idea.

The incautious security of the citizens of Philadelphia, at the first stage of the disorder, is highly to be regretted. Most of those who died of the malignant disorder, before the 26th of August, were carried to burial with the accustomed parade of attendants which so generally prevails in this city. The chief of the persons who at that time carried the dead to the grave, and several of those who attended the funerals, were speedily taken sick, and hurried into eternity.

Sebastian Ale, an old grave-digger, who had long lost the sense of smelling, fancied he could not take the disorder, and followed his business without apprehension. A husband and his wife who lay sick together, wished to be interred in the same grave. Their deaths happened within a few days of each other. When the latter of the two was to be buried, Sebastian was employed to dig open the other's grave. He struck upon and broke the coffin, and in stooping down, received into his mouth such an intolerable and deadly stench, that he was taken sick immediately, and in a day or two died.

The scourge of the yellow fever has fallen with extreme severity on some families. There are various instances of five and six, and some of eight, ten, and of Godfrey Gebler's family no less than eleven were swept off the face of the earth. Dr. Sproat, his wife, son, and daughter—Michael Hay, his wife, and three children—David Fliekwir and five of his family—Samuel Weatherby, wife, and four grown children, are no more. And there are numberless instances of a havoc equally great in particular families. There is one house in this city, from which above twenty perfons were carried, fome to Bufhhill, but the moft of them to the grave.

There is one fact refpecting this diforder, which renders it probable, that the exercife of the duties of humanity towards the fugitive Philadelphians, would not have been attended with the danger univerfally imagined. In defiance of all the refolutions entered into by the inhabitants of various towns, many of our infected citizens evaded their vigilance, and took refuge among them; and in very few cafes is it known that they communicated the infection.—Three perfons died of this diforder, in one houfe near Woodbury, in New Jerfey; they had been attended during their illnefs, by the family, none of whom caught the difeafe. Six or feven died at Darby, as many at Germantown, and eight at Haddonfield, without communicating it to any of the inhabitants. A man from Philadelphia, of the name of Cornell, died in New York, about two days after his arrival. The place of his death was a boarding houfe, in which were feveral boarders, one of whom flept in the fame bed with him. Two of the family only were flightly affected—but not in fuch a degree as to require medical aid. Several other infected perfons from our city, died there, and no one caught the infection from them. A man died at one of the principal taverns in Baltimore, of the fame diforder. Many people had vifited and attended him during the whole of his illnefs, without injury. No perfon was affected but his doctor, whofe indifpofition was not of long continuance. A great number of fimilar inftances have occurred at Burlington, Bordenton, Lamberton, Princeton, Brunfwic, Woodbridge, Newark, Lancafter, and various other places.

Since the firft edition appeared, I have had information from a number of creditable perfons, that the idea that the diforder has not been communicated out of Philadelphia, is erroneous. A family, of the name of Hopper, near Woodbury, took it from fome of our infected citizens, and three of them died. A woman in Chester county, who had boarded and lodged some of the sick, died of the malignant fever. Three people, of one family in Trenton, took it from a sick person from Philadelphia, and died of it. A negro servant belonging to mr. Morgan, of Pensaucon creek, in New Jersey, took up an infected bed floating in the Delaware, which spread the disorder in the family, and mrs. Morgan and her girl both died of it. It was introduced by his son from Philadelphia, into the family of mr. Cadwallader, at Abington, some of whom died with it. Some others in different places caught the infection, and died. But the cases of this kind have been extremely few, considering the numbers, who carried the disorder from hence, and died with it in the country.

C H A P. XVII. *Another collection of scraps.*

THOSE who reflect on the many shocking cases of cruelty and desertion of friends and relations which occurred in Philadelphia, however they may regret, cannot be surprised, that in the country, and in various towns and cities, inhumanity should be experienced by Philadelphians, from strangers. The universal consternation extinguished in people's breasts the most honourable feelings of human nature ; and in this case, as in various others, the suspicion operated as injuriously as the reality. Many travellers from this city, exhausted with fatigue and with hunger, have been refused shelter and sustenance, and have fallen victims to the fears, not to the want of charity, of those to whom they applied for relief*. Instances of this kind have occurred on almost every road leading from Philadelphia. People under suspicion of having this disorder, have been forced by their fellow travellers to quit the stages, and perished in the woods without a possibility of procuring any assistance. At Easton, in Maryland, a waggon-load of goods from Philadel-

* The fugitive Philadelphians were in general as strict in their precautions against them who fled later than they, as any of the country people.

phia was actually burned; and a woman, who came with it, was, it is said, tarred and feathered!

In a town in Jersey, an association was entered into to prevent all intercourse with Philadelphia, and the inhabitants agreed, to mount guard, alternately. One man, who was principled against this severity, refused to do duty, or join in the combination. He was advertised, and all people forbidden to have any communication with him—indeed he was absolutely refused the necessaries of life—a butcher, who passed his door, told him, when applied to for provisions, that he had meat enough, but none for him. Having gone, for a short time, from home, in the direction towards Philadelphia, but not within thirty miles of the city, the centinel on duty stopped him on his return—and he persisting in his determination to proceed, the other presented his firelock, and it is supposed would have shot him, but for the interference of a third person.

The son of a citizen of Philadelphia arrived at a town in Virginia fourteen days before the time of fixing the quarantine, which was for twenty days. However, he was still obliged to undergo the full quarantine after that time, which made thirty-four days, exclusive of above six days spent on the road.

An emigrant from Philadelphia, who had been away nearly three weeks, had to cross a ferry in a neighbouring state, and was provided with proper certificates of the length of time he was absent. He got into the scow, with his wife, and carriage, and was rowed over to the opposite side. There he was refused permission to land, as he had not a certificate from a particular magistrate in that part of the country. He leaped out of the scow, on a rock, and the centinel swore he would blow his brains out, if he advanced a step farther. His wife, who was in the boat, was under the most dreadful apprehensions, as the ferrymen were drunk, the horses in the carriage fretful, and the wind high. In fpite of his intreaties, and his offers to prove the length of his abfence, he was obliged to return in queft of the magiftrate pointed out. When he arrived at his houfe, which was feveral miles from the ferry, the juftice concealed himfelf, though fear of catching the diforder. He then went to another, fome miles further back. By the time he returned to the ferry, it was nine o'clock, and he had to wait till next morning.

A poor man was taken fick on the road at a village not far from Philadelphia. He lay calling for water, a confiderable time in vain. At length, an old woman brought a pitcher full, and not daring to approach him, fhe laid it at a diftance, defiring him to crawl to it, which he did. After lying there about forty-eight hours, he died; and the body lay in a ftate of putrefaction for fome time, until the neighbours hired two black butchers to bury him, for twenty-four dollars: They dug a pit to windward—with a fork, hooked a rope about his neck---dragged him into it---and, at as great a diftance as poffible, caft earth into the pit to cover him.

One of our citizens loft his brother in the country, with the malignant fever ; and, owing to the fears of the neighbours, could not prevail on any perfon even to make him a coffin. He was obliged to wrap him up in a blanket, to dig a grave for him, and bury him with his own hands.

In a fmall town not far diftant from Philadelphia, very arbitrary attempts were unfeelingly made to oblige one of our fugitives to mount guard againft his own fellow citizens. He refufed ; and finding him refolute againft every effort, they were obliged to defift.

In one of the American ports, a Philadelphia veffel, juft arrived, was forced to return to fea with only two gallons of water for each man. In the fame port, one of the captains from our city had his boat ftove to pieces.

***

The 17th of September, the weftern fhore Baltimore ftage was ftopped about two miles from that town, by an armed guard. The hour of arrival was about eight o'clock at night. There was a tavern at piftol-fhot from the place. But the tavern keeper refufed to receive the paffengers, twelve in number. They were detained on the road all night without any fhelter but the ftage, in which they dozed a part of the night; during the remainder of it, they lay before a fire which they had kindled in the woods. Next morning, the tavern-keeper, one Murray, an inhuman Goth, when they fent to him for breakfaft, refufed to give them any. But about two hours afterwards, he let them have fome bread, cheefe, wine, and cider, with which they breakfafted on the road. In this fitu-ation they remained until the afternoon, that is, for eighteen hours. A captain in the French navy, with his wife, and feveral French gentlemen, were among the paffengers,

***

A refpectable citizen of Philadelphia left the city on the 17th of September, intending to refide on Long Ifland till the diforder ceafed. He was taken ill on the road—and prevented from proceeding, near Newark. He took lodgings at a captain Littel's near Second river. The alarm fpread of an infected man being in the houfe—the neighbours affembled—fixed a fence on each fide of Littel's houfe, and obliged the people to remove out of a houfe near to it, which the fence likewife enclofed. The road and river lay before Littel's door; the former was entirely cut off by the fence, which run clear to the river. At the diftance of a hundred yards, was a church, in which public worfhip was intermitted for three or four weeks, through fear. Travellers took a circuitous route of above a mile, to avoid danger.

At length he died—and his fon, about nine years old, had to affift in performing the laft melancholy rites for him. The fence remained for ten days after his death, to afcertain whether or not his family had taken the diforder.

Juftice requires me to add, that they were not fuffered to be in want of any neceffaries. They were directed to write what they had occafion for, on a paper and faften it on the fence. Perfons were appointed to fupply them with whatever was requifite.

An artful girl, juft from Philadelphia, completely deceived the centinel ftationed near Bordentown. She afked him, with much earneftnefs, as if afraid to venture in, was *that there* confounded yellow fever got into the town?—" No," fays he, " you may go in with as much fafety as to your own home." I need not add, that fhe went forward.

A Philadelphian, in a fmall town near this city, loft his child in the fever, and went to bury it. On his return, he found all his furniture on the road, and the doors locked : and no intreaties could again procure him admittance.

When tar was in ufe among the various preventatives, a boy was determined to fecure himfelf by night as well as by day ; and accordingly tied a tarred rope twice about his neck, and afterwards buttoned his collar with fome difficulty. He woke in the night, half ftrangled, and black in the face. He may with juftice be faid to have nearly choaked himfelf, to fave his life.

It would be extraordinary if fo very favourable an opportunity of inventing marvellous ftories, fhould have been fuffered to pafs over without fome prodigies being recorded. Mankind are ever prone to the

Extravagant, especially when their passions are warmed. And pity and terror, two passions particularly calculated to foster this disposition, being roused into action to the highest degree, the marvellous stories, which were every where current, and which even stole into print, can be easily accounted for. Some of the Maryland papers relate, that " a voice had been heard in the streets of Philadelphia, warning the inhabitants to prepare for their doom, as written in the prophet Ezekiel, ch. 27." The Marylander who heard this voice, was certainly gifted with a most extraordinary ear, as, at the distance of above a hundred miles, he heard what we could not hear on the spot. And it would appear that his *sight* was equally good with his hearing ; for he *saw* two angels conversing with the watch. It is true, he is too modest to say, he saw them himself—he only says " two angels were *seen* conversing with the watch at midnight, about the subject of what the voice had previously proclaimed." But no person here having ever seen them—it is fairly presumable, as it would be highly criminal to doubt of facts resting on such authority, that, he must have been the eye-witness himself.

A merchant of Philadelphia, who had been absent for several weeks, was returning to the city in the second week of November, having heard that the danger was no more. He met a man on the road going from Philadelphia ; and naturally enquired into the state of affairs. The other told him, that a coffin maker, who had been employed by the committee for relief of the sick, had found such a decrease of demand two weeks before, that he had a large supply of coffins on hand ; but that the mortality had again so far increased, that he had sold all, and had seven journeymen employed day and night. This so alarmed the Philadelphian, that he again returned with his family, to wait a more favourable issue.

A drunken failor lay in the ftreet, in the northern liberties, for a few hours afleep, and was fuppofed by the neighbours to be dead with the diforder ; but they were too much afraid, to make perfonal examination. They fent to the committee at the city hall for a cart and a coffin. The carter took the man by the heels, and was going to put him into the coffin. Handling him roughly, he awoke, and damning his eyes, alked him what he was about? the carter let him drop in a fright, and ran off as if a ghoft was at his heels.

❦❦❧❦❦❧❦❦

A lunatic, who had the malignant fever, was advifed, by his neighbours, to go to Bufhhill. He confented, and got into the cart ; but foon changing his mind, he flipt out at the end, unknown to the carter, who, after a while, miffing him, and feeing him at a diftance running away, turned his horfe about, and trotted hard after him. The other doubled his pace ; and the carter whipped his horfe to a gallop ; but the man turned a corner, and hid himfelf in a houfe, leaving the mortified carter to return, and deliver an account of his ludicrous adventure.

❦❦❧❦❦❧❦❦

Several inftances have occurred of the carters on their arrival at Bufhhill, and proceeding to deliver up their charge, finding, to their amazement, the carts empty.

❦❦❧❦❦❧❦❦

A woman, whofe hufband died, refufed to have him buried in a coffin provided for her by one of her friends, as too paltry and mean. She bought an elegant and coftly one—and had the other laid by in the yard. In a week, fhe was herfelf a corpfe—and was buried in the very coffin fhe had fo much defpifed.

❦❦❧❦❦❧❦❦

The wife of a man who lived in Walnut-ftreet, was feized with the malignant fever, and given over by the doctors. The hufband abandoned her, and next night lay out of the houfe for fear of catching the infection. In the morning, taking it for granted, from the very low ftate fhe had been in, that fhe was dead, he purchafed a coffin for her; but on entering the houfe, was furprifed to fee her much recovered. He fell fick fhortly after, died, and was buried in the very coffin, which he had fo precipitately bought for his wife, who is ftill living.

The powers of the god of love might be imagined to lie dormant amidft fuch fcenes of diftrefs as Bufh-hill exhibited. But we find that his fway was felt there with equal force as any where elfe. John John-fon, and Prifcilla Hicks, two of the patients, who had recovered, and officiated as nurfes to the fick, were fmitten with each other's charms—and, procuring leave of abfence for an hour or two, they came to the city on the 23d of September, were joined in the bands of matrimony, and returned to their avocation at the hofpital. A long chafm took place in the hymeneal re-cords; for no adventure of the fame kind occurred, until the 5th of November, when Naffy, a Portu-guefe mulatto, took to wife Hannah Smith, a bouncing German girl, who, as well as himfelf, was employed as nurfe.

The ftate of the police and of fociety in Philadel-phia, appears to no fmall advantage, when we confider one circumftance. Notwithftanding the abfence of the magiftrates, and the immenfe value of property left unprotected through the fears of the owners, and the deaths of the perfons left to take care of it, there was only one or two burglaries committed.—One was at-tempted: but the rogues were difcovered and taken. A hardened villain from a neighbouring ftate, formed a plot with fome negroes to plunder houfes. He was a mafter rogue, had digefted a complete fyftem, and formed a large partnerfhip for the more fuccefsful ex-ecution of his fchemes. However, he was foon feized, and the company diffolved.

M

The jail of Philadelphia is under such excellent re.
gulation, that the diforder made its appearance there
only in two or three inftances, although fuch abodes
of mifery are the places where contagious diforders are
moft commonly generated. When the yellow fever
raged moft violently in the city, there were in the
jail one hundred and fix French foldiers and failors,
confined by order of the French conful ; befides eighty
convicts, vagrants, and perfons for trial ; all of whom,
except two or three, remained perfectly free from the
complant. Several circumftances confpired to produce
this falutary effect. The people confined were frequent.
ly cleanfed and purified by the ufe of the cold bath
—they were kept conftantly employed—vegetables
formed a confiderable part of their diet—in the yard,
vegetation flourifhed—and many of them being employed in ftone-cutting, the water, conftantly running,
kept the atmofphere in a moift ftate, while the peo.
ple of Philadelphia were almoft uninterruptedly
parched up by unceafing heat. Elijah Weed, the
late jailor, caught the diforder in the city, and died
in the jail, without communicating it to any of the
people confined. I hope I fhall be excufed for paying a
tribute to the memory of this valuable citizen, under
whofe government of the jail, and with whofe hearty
co-operation, moft of the regulations in that inftitution have been effected, which, with the fuccefsful
experiments made in England, prove that jails may
be eafily converted from finks of human depravity
and wretchednefs, into places of reformation ; fo that,
inftead of rendering the idle vagrant, confined
merely on fufpicion, or for want of friends to protect
him, obdurate, wicked, and ripe for rapine and fpoil,
—the profligate and abandoned may be fo reclaimed
in them, as, on their liberation, to become ufeful
members of fociety. For the honour of human nature,
it ought to be recorded, that fome of the convicts
in the jail, a part of the term of whofe confinement
had been remitted, as a reward for their peaceable, or-
derly behaviour, voluntarily offered themfelves as
nurfes, to attend the fick at Bufh-hill, and have in

that capacity conducted themfelves with great fidelity. Among them are fome who were formerly regarded, and with juftice, as hardened, abandoned villains, which the old fyftem ufually rendered every tenant of a jail, who remained there a few weeks. According to the fame fummary fyftem, thefe men's lives would have been long fince offered up as an atonement to fociety for the injury they had done it. That is, in plain Englifh, becaufe fociety had fuffered one injury by rapine, it was neceffary it fhould fuffer another by law. But by the prefent improved and humane plan, they and great numbers of others are reftored to fociety and ufefulnefs once more. So much better, although a little more troublefome, is it, to reform men, than to butcher them under colour of law and juftice.

<hr />

The fympathy for our calamities, difplayed in various places, and the very liberal contributions raifed for our relief, reflect the higheft honour on their inhabitants, and demand our warmeft gratitude. The inhabitants of Gloucefter county, in New Jerfey, have the honour of being firft in this laudable race. So early as the 30th of September, they had a confiderable fum collected, with which they purchafed a quantity of provifions for the ufe of the hofpital at Bufh-hill. They have, from that time, regularly continued copious fupplies twice a week. In addition to this, they have made, and are now making, confiderable purchafes of wood, for the relief of the poor during the winter. From a few citizens of Philadelphia, near Germantown, there have been received two thoufand dollars; from others near Darby, fourteen hundred; from New York, five thoufand; from a perfon unknown, five hundred; from Bucks' county, fixteen hundred; from Delaware county, twelve hundred; from Franklin county, nearly five hundred; from Bofton, fundry articles, which have been fold for nearly two thoufand; and from fundry other perfons and places, contributions equally liberal and honourable.

There has been a very ftrong analogy between the ftate of Philadelphia, and that of an army. About the clofe of Auguft, and till the middle of September, when the dangers were few, and, by prudent management, might have been eafily furmounted, an univerfal trepidation benumbed people's faculties; and flight and felf-prefervation feemed to engrofs the whole attention of a large proportion of the citizens. Juft fo, with an army of recruits. Every breath of wind terrifies them. Vague rumours are heard with fear and trembling. In every tree at a diftance is beheld a formidable enemy, to whom they are ready to lay down their arms, and furrender at difcretion. But when the " din of arms, and cannon's rattle" have familiarized them with the horrid trade of death, the obftinate phalanx beholds, unmoved, its ranks mowed down, and death advancing, with rapid ftrides, to terminate their (as it is falfely termed) *glorious* career. —Even thus was it here. Towards the clofe of September, and during the firft part of October, when the horrors of the fcene were conftantly increafing, and from fifty to a hundred were interred daily, then people caft away their various preventatives—thieves' vinegar, tarred ropes, garlic, camphor bags, fmelling bottles, &c.—And then it was, that they affumed a manly fortitude, tempered with the fober, ferious penfivenefs, befitting fuch an awful fcene.

A friend, to whom I communicated this idea, has endeavoured to explain the matter differently. He fays, that thofe who were terrified at firft, generally fled away—and left behind fuch as were poffeffed of a ftronger frame of mind. This is an error; as many men, who were among the moft ftriking inftances of the influence of terror at firft, behaved, in the end, with the moft exemplary fortitude.

Shall I be pardoned for paffing a cenfure on thofe, whofe miftaken zeal led them, during the moft dreadful ftages of the calamity, to croud fome of our churches, and aid this frightful enemy in his work of deftruction? who, fearful, left their prayers and adoration at home would not find acceptance before the Deity, reforted to churches filled with bodies of contagious air, where, with every breath, they inhaled noxious miafmata? To this fingle caufe I am bold in afcribing a large proportion of the mortality—And it is remarkable, that thofe congregations, whofe places of worfhip were moft crouded, have fuffered the moft dreadfully. Will men never acquire wifdom? Are we yet to learn, that the Almighty architect of the heavens and earth, does not require " temples " made with men's hands?" that going to a place of worfhip, againft the great law of felf-prefervation, implanted in indelible characters by his divine hand, on the breaft of every one of his creatures, conftitutes no part of the adoration due to the maker and prefer. ver of mankind? That a " meek and humble heart" is the temple wherein he delights to be worfhipped ? I hope not—I hope the awful leffon fome of our congregations hold forth on this fubject, by a mortality out of all proportion to their numbers, will ferve as a memento, at all future times, in the like critical emergencies !*

—◁◐▷—

Some of thofe who remained in the city, have, for reafons not very eafy to juftify, been in the habit of reproaching thofe who fled, with criminality, as deferters, who abandoned their pofts†. I believe, on the

---

* This paragraph, although erroneous, is retained, that I may have an opportunity, which I chearfully embrace, of acknowledging the miftake I have committed. On a revifion of the bills of mortality, it appears, that thofe congregations who kept up religious worfhip regularly, did not lofe more than, and fome not fo many as, their ufual proportions. In one year, ending July 31, 1793, the German Lutherans buried more than a fixth of the whole number of the dead in the city—the German reformed, a fifteenth—the Friends, a tenth—and St. Mary's, an eighth. From Auguft 1, to Nov. 9, 1793, the burials among the German Lutherans were not quite a fixth—among the German Reformed, nearly a fixteenth—among the Friends, an eleventh— and in St. Mary's grave-yard, a fixteenth. Thefe were the congregations I alluded to, in the above remarks.

† If they were even guilty of a crime, it brought its own punifhment; as I am fully convinced, that thofe who were abfent, and a prey to the anxiety caufed by the frightful reports current, fuffered as much as thofe who remained in the city.

contrary, that as the nature of our government, did not allow the arbitrary measures to be pursued, which, in despotic countries, would probably have extinguished the disorder at an early period—it was the duty of every person to avoid the danger, whose circumstances and situation allowed it. The effects of the desertion were, moreover, salutary*. The sphere of action of the disorder was diminished. Two or three empty houses arrested the disease in its progress, as it was slowly, but surely travelling through a street, and probably rescued a neighbourhood from its ravages. We shall long have to mourn the severe loss our city has felt, in being bereft of so many valuable citizens: and had the 17,000, who retired, been in the city during the prevalence of the disorder, and lost as large a proportion of their number, as those did who remained, we should, instead of 4000 dead, have lost nearly 6000; and perhaps had to deplore in the number, another Clow, a Cay, a Lea, a Sims, a Dunkin, a Strawbridge, men of extensive business, whose loss will be long felt—a Pennington, a Glentworth, a Hutchinson, a Sargeant, a Howell, a Waring, men endowed by heaven with eminent abilities—a Fleming, a Graefsl, a Sproat, men of exalted piety and virtue—a Wilson, an Adgate, a Baldwin, a Carroll, a Tomkins, an Offley, citizens of most estimable characters. Let those then who have remained, regard their long-absent friends, as if preserved from death by their flight, and rejoice at their return in health and safety. Let those who have been absent, acknowledge the exertions of those who maintained their ground. Let us all unite in the utmost vigilance to prevent the return of this fell destroyer, by the most scrupulous attention to cleansing and purifying our scourged city—and let us join in thanksgiving to that Supreme Being, who has, in his own time, stayed the avenging storm, ready to devour us, after it had laughed to scorn all human efforts.

* Perhaps had all our citizens remained, famine would have been added to our calamity ; whereas, the markets were abundantly supplied during the whole time. The prices, too, were, in general not far beyond what they usually are at the same season of the year.

Committee for relieving the sick and distressed, appointed by a meeting of the citizens of Philadelphia, summoned by advertisement in the public papers, Sept. 13, 1793.

PRESIDENT.
Matthew Clarkson
SECRETARY.
Caleb Lownes.
TREASURER.
Thomas Wistar.
MANAGERS OF BUSHHILL HOSPITAL.
Stephen Girard.
Peter Helm.
ORPHAN COMMITTEE.
Israel Israel.
John Letchworth.
James Kerr.
James Sharswood.
COMMITTEE OF DISTRIBUTION.
Israel Israel.
John Haworth.
James Swaine.
Mathew Carey.
Thomas Savery.
James Kerr.
Jacob Witman.

John Letchworth.
James Sharswood.
Samuel Benge.
SUPERINTENDANT OF THE BURIALS
OF THE DEAD, AND REMOVAL OF
THE SICK.
Samuel Benge.
DISTRIBUTOR OF SUPPLIES.
Henry Deforest.
COMMITTEE OF ACCOUNTS.
James Sharswood.
John Conelly.
COMMITTEE ON THE PUBLICATION
OF LETTERS.
Caleb Lownes.
Mathew Carey.
DECEASED MEMBERS.
Andrew Adgate.
J. D Sargeant.
Daniel Offley.
Joseph Inskeep.

Assistant committee, chosen October 14.

SAMUEL COATES, Chairman.

JOHN OLDDEN, Secretary.

Northern Liberties.
William Peter Spragues.
William Gregory.
Jacob Witman.
James Swaine.
Joseph Burns.
George Forepaugh.
Casper Snyder.
Peter Smith.
Vine to Race street.
Richard Whitehead.
Joseph Kerr.
John Ettries.
Race to Arch.
Thomas Willis.
Daniel Dawson.
Peter Thomson.
Thomas Allibone.
Lambert Wilmer.
Arch to Market.
William Sansom.
Justinian Fox.
Amos Wickersham.
Market to Chesnut.
Arthur Howell.
Alexander Cochran.
Thomas Dobson.

Chesnut to Walnut.
Jeremiah Paul.
James Cummins.
Casper W. Morris.
Thomas Castiere.
Walnut to Spruce.
George Rutter.
Benjamin W. Morris.
Spruce to Pine.
Samuel Pancoast, jun.
John Woodside.
Levi Hollingsworth.
William Watkins.
Pine to South.
John Wood.
Adam Brittle.
William Eckard.
Thomas Dicksey.
Fergus M'Elwaine.
Southwark.
William Innis.
Richard Mosely.
William Robinson, sen.
John Grantham.
John Savadge.
John Pattison.

APPENDIX.——No. I.

An account of the plague in London, in the year 1665.

ABOUT the clofe of the year 1664, the plague was brought over to London in fome Levant goods, that came from Holland.

The narrownefs of the ftreets and lanes in London, the clofenefs of the houfes, and their being crouded with families, rendered the inhabitants very liable to fuffer by infectious diforders in fickly feafons ; and the plague was almoft continually among the difeafes enumerated in the bills of mortality. The goods above mentioned, were carried to a houfe in Long-acre, near Drury-Lane, where they were firft opened. Here two Frenchmen died ; the diforder communicated to other houfes in the neighbourhood, and infected the parifh officers who were employed about the dead. Ano- lived near the infected houfes, removed, fo . to Bearbinder-lane, where he died : and thus the plague got into the city.

The further progrefs of this cruel diforder was ftopped during a hard froft which fet in this winter, and continued till March, 1665,—when its virulence was revived, by the advance of the fpring. At firft it feized one here, then another a mile or more diftant, after which it appeared again where it was obferved before, juft as accident furnifhed it with conveyance, and according to the time when perfons contracted the diftemper.

The ufual fymptoms of infection, for it is not propofed to enter into a ftr fideration of the plague, are thus enumerated by dr. Hodges, who lived then in London, and attended patients in all ftages of the diforder. Firft, a horror, vomiting, delirium, dizzinefs, head-ach, and ftupefaction ; then a fever, watching, palpitation of the heart, bleeding, at the nofe, and a great heat about the præcordia : but the figns more peculiar to the peftilence, were, thofe puftules, which the common people called blains,

buboes, carbuncles, fpots, and thofe marks called tokens. The buboes were hard, painful tumours, with
inflammation and gatherings upon the glands, behind
the ears, the armpits, and the groin. Thefe tumours,
at their firft appearance, were hard, and the event of
the diforder was prognofticated from their fudden
or flow increafe, from their genuine or untoward fup-
puration, and from the virulence of their contents.
The peftilential fpots appeared chiefly on the neck,
breaft, and back, and were not eafily diftinguifhable
from flea-bites. The genuine peftilential characters,
commonly called tokens, as being the forewarnings
of death, were minute diftinct blafts, which had their
origin from within, and rofe up in little pyramidal
protuberances, fometimes as fmall as pin-heads, other
times as large as a filver penny, having the peftilential
poifon chiefly collected at their bafes, gradually taint-
ing the neighbouring parts, and reaching the furface
as the configuration of the veffels and pores favoured
their fpreading. They were alfo derivable from external caufes, as from the injuries of air, when the peftilential *miafmata* were pent up and condenfed; and
by that means their virulence increafed, fo that life
was immediately extinguifhed when they reached the
noble organs.

In the treatment of the fick, all the phyficians agreed
in throwing out the peftilential malignity as foon as
poffible by alexipharmics, and to thefe, as foon as the
belly was loofened, recourfe was had as to a facred refuge: in extremity fome had recourfe to mineral pre-
parations, as mineral *bezoar, fulphur auratum, aura vitæ,*
&c. in order to drive out the peftilence by mere
force. For external applications, they ufed blifters
and cataplafms; the buboes were opened by incifion;
and the efchar formed by the virulent ichor, difcharged
by the carbuncles, was chiefly got off by actual caute-
ry; nor were the blifters, ulcers, or incifions, fuffered to heal until the malignity of the difeafe was fpent.
But fuch was the delufory appearance of this peftilence,
that many patients were loft, when they were thought
in fafe recovery; whereas, others furvived, who were

N

given over for loft, much to the difcredit of the medical art.

The apprehenfions of the people were greatly increafed, by the crafty predictions of fortune-tellers,
cunning-men, aftrologers, and quacks, who hung out
their figns in every ftreet, and found their account
in heightening the general terror; nor was their trade
ftopped, until thefe men of fuperior knowledge in
the decrees of providence, were themfelves fwept
away in the common calamity. As foon as the magiftrates found that the contagion extended into feveral parifhes, an order was iffued for fhutting up infected houfes, to ftop the communication of the diforder. Thefe houfes had red croffes painted on the doors,
with this infcription, *Lord, have mercy upon us!* and
watchmen were placed before them, who were daily
relieved, to hand neceffaries and medicines into the
confined families, and to reftrain them from coming
abroad until forty days after recovery. But though
thefe regulations were ftrictly executed, the propriety
of them was much controverted, and the hardfhip univerfally complained of; for if a frefh perfon was feized
in the fame houfe, but a day before this quarantine
expired, it was again renewed; which intolerable te-
dious imprifonment of the healthy with the fick, frequently ended with the deaths of whole families. Neither did this confinement of the fick prove effectual;
for each houfe having but one guard, and many houfes
having avenues behind, it was impoffible to fecure all
paffages; fo that, fome would amufe the watchmen
with difcourfe on one fide of the houfe, while the reft
of the family made their efcape at the other; until, at
length, the men were left to watch empty houfes.
Some watchmen were publicly whipped through the
ftreets, for taking bribes to let perfons out privately;
and where fuch opportunities did not offer, the watchmen were fometimes ill treated: one near Coleman-
ftreet was blown up by gunpowder; and while he lay
difabled by the explofion, thofe who had ftrength,
efcaped out of the houfe. Some perfons alfo would let
themfelves down from the windows, armed with fwords

and piftols, in the fight of the watchmen, and threaten them with inftant death, if they called out or ftirred. Many of them were even killed in difputes with thofe they were charged with the care of guarding.

It is a fad, though true character of human nature, to remark, that there are always mifcreants ready to take advantage of public calamities; and what greatly contributed to the lofs of perfons thus fhut up, was the villainous behaviour of fome nurfes. Thefe wretches from an inhuman greedinefs to plunder the dead, would not only ftrangle their patients, and charge their deaths to the diftemper in their throats; but would fecretly convey the peftilential taint from the fores of the fick to thofe who were well. Yet though they were without witneffes in thefe diabolical practices, they often fell themfelves the juft victims of their own unguarded prefumption.

Dogs and cats, being domeftic animals, apt to run from houfe to houfe, and being fuppofed to convey the noxious effluvia in their fur or hair; an early order was made by the lord-mayor and other magiftrates, by the advice of the phyficians, that they fhould all be immediately killed; and an officer was appointed for that purpofe. It was computed that 40,000 dogs, and five times as many cats, were maffacred in confequence of this prefcription; and all poffible endeavours were ufed to exterminate rats and mice by poifon, on the fame account.

It was inconceivable, as the plague increafed, with what precipitation fuch inhabitants of the city as were able to leave it, deferted into the country; for fome weeks it was difficult to get to the lord-mayor's door, for the throngs that crouded in to get paffes and certificates of health; without which none were permitted to travel through, or lodge in, any towns on the road. The nobility, gentry, and richer tradefmen retired firft, and in the broad ftreets leading out of town, nothing was to be feen but waggons and carts loaded with goods, and fervants; coaches full of families—and horfemen, all hurrying away; with empty carriages returning for frefh loads.

Some families that had no country retreats, laid up a ftore of provifions, and fhut themfelves up fo carefully, as not to be heard of nor feen, until the plague ceafed; when they came abroad fafe and well;—among thefe were feveral Dutch merchants, who kept their houfes like garrifons befieged, fuffering no one to go out or come in, and thus preferved themfelves in health. —Many merchants and fhip owners fhut themfelves up on board fhips, and as the plague increafed, removed down the river, nor was it heard that the diforder reached any veffels below Deptford. Poorer perfons took refuge in hoys, fmacks, and fifhing boats; but thefe took the infection; others went up the river in boats, lodging by night in tents made of their fails, on fhore; for though the country people would fupply them with provifions, they would not receive them into their houfes. The poor who ran abroad in their extremities into the country, were often ill ufed and driven back, which caufed great exclamation againft the cruelty of the country towns; but felf-prefervation extinguifhed humanity; and yet notwithftanding all their care, there was not a town within twenty miles but fuffered more or lefs by the diforder.

Thus the diftemper was felt chiefly to prey on the common people; which it did to fuch a degree as to obtain the name of the *poor's plague*. The lord-mayor, fheriffs, aldermen, or their deputies, with many of the common council, very humanely to compofe the minds of the people as much as poffible, publifhed their refolution not to quit the city; but to be always ready at hand to preferve order, and to do juftice on all occafions. The lord-mayor held councils every day, making neceffary difpofitions for preferving the public peace; the people were treated with all the gentlenefs circumftances would allow, while prefumptuous rogues, houfebreakers, and plunderers of the fick or dead, were duly punifhed, and fevere declarations iffued againft them.

It was one of their principal concerns to fee the regulations for the freedom and good fupply of the markets, obferved—and every market-day the lord-mayor, Sir John Lawrence, or the fheriffs, attended vigilantly on horfeback, to fee their orders executed. The neceffity of going to market was greatly contributory to the ruin of the city, as there the people caught the infection one of another, and it was fufpected that even the provifions were tainted; all imaginable precautions were however ufed in thefe negociations—for cuftomers took the meat from off the hooks themfelves, that they might not receive it from the butcher—and for his fecurity dropped their money into pans of vinegar, always carrying fmall money with them, that they might receive no change. Every one that could procure them, carried fcents and perfumes about them, while the pooreft inhabitants were forced on all occafions to run all hazards.

The infection, notwithftanding every caution, continued through the months of May and June, with more or lefs feverity—fometimes raging in one part, and then in another—about the latter end of June, above twenty parifhes were infected, and the King removed from Whitehall to Hampton court. Government was not however inattentive to the diftreffes of the metropolis—for befide appointing a monthly faft for public prayer, the king commanded the college of phyficians to compofe and publifh an Englifh directory of general advice in this calamitous feafon. Some of the college were appointed to attend the fick on all occafions; and two out of the court of aldermen were required to fee this hazardous duty performed: nor were there eminent phyficians wanting who voluntarily and courageoufly gave their affiftance in fo dangerous an employment; eight or nine of whom were deftroyed in the duty.

In the firft week of July, the bill rofe to 725, the next week to 1089, the third week to 1843, and the next week to 2010. About the middle of the month, the diforder, which had chiefly raged in St. Giles's Holburn, and toward Weftminfter, began to travel eaftward, and over the river to Lambeth and Southwark; but kept principally in the out parifhes which were fulleft of poor. When it abated in the weftern parifhes, it exerted its violence in Clerkenwell, Cripplegate, Shoreditch, Bifhopfgate, Alderfgate, Whitechapel and Stepney. In the months of Auguft and September the diforder made moft terrible flaughter;

three, four, or five thoufand died in a week, the deaths one week amounted to 8,000 and were believed to extend to 10,000! for the regifters in fuch confufion were not kept with great accuracy.

Under thefe fhocking circumftances, when the people were in the greateft want of fpiritual confolation, they were in general forfaken by their parochial minifters; and fad as the minds of the people were, there were not wanting fome who fatirized them in lampoons, for this fcandalous defertion of their diftreffed flocks. When on fome church doors were written, *Here is a pulpit to let*, and on others, *A pulpit to be fold*, then it was that the ejected non-conforming minifters, fhowed that difinterefted concern for the people, that conftitutes the true effence of the clerical character; for, unmindful of their legal difability, and regardlefs of the furrounding danger, they refolutely mounted the vacant pulpits, often twice a day, and foothed the griefs of crouded audiences by their pious difcourfes and other religious exercifes.

When deaths became fo numerous, the church yards were unable to contain the bodies, and the ufual modes of interment were no longer obferved: occafional pits of great extent were dug in feveral parts, to which the dead were brought by cart-loads, collected by the ring of a bell, and the doleful cry of *Bring out your dead!* They were put into the carts with no other covering than rugs or fheets tied round them by their friends, if they had any furviving; and were fhot down in promifcuous heaps! Sometimes the drivers of thofe carts would drop in their employments, and the carts would be found without any conductor; in the parifh of Stepney, it was faid they loft within the year, 116 fextons, grave-diggers and their affiftants!

Trade was at a ftand, fhops were fhut up, every day looked like a folemn Sabbath; few were to be feen in the ftreets, and neither cart nor coach appeared but fuch as were employed for immediate acts of neceffity: grafs grew in the moft public ftreets, and in the Royal-Exchange,—and the broad ftreet in Whitechapel might be miftaken for a green field. Thofe families who carried on retail trades, or fubfifted by labour, were now fup-

ported by charity, which is recorded to have been wor-
thily extended by those who had ability to bestow it.
The king contributed 1000l. a week, and dr. Sheldon,
archbishop of Canterbury, who remained at Lambeth
the whole time, beside his own benefactions, procured
great sums to be remitted from the diocefes under his
jurisdiction, by his affecting letters to the bishops—
Monk, afterwards duke of Albemarle, with lord Craven,
remained in London, and exerted all their abilities to al-
leviate the distresses they were witness to. Though the
city was in general abandoned by the rich, yet these did
not forget those who were left behind—large sums were
fent up by them to the magistrates, as well as from the
trading towns in the remotest parts of England. The
degree of general distress in the metropolis may be fuppofed void of exaggeration, when it is said that beside
private charities, the lord mayor and aldermen were
enabled to bestow 100,000l. a week for several weeks
together to the poor!

That nothing might be left untried to disperse the
contagion, large fires were ordered to be made in the
public streets; yet the physicians were very diffident of
the success of this expensive experiment; and the trial
foon decided in favour of their doubts. Coals were then
4l. per chaldron; and two hundred chaldron were applied in making fires at the custom-house, Billingsgate,
at the bridge-foot, three cranes, Queenhithe, Bridewell-
gate, the corner of Leadenhall and Grace church streets,
at the north and fouth gates of the Royal Exchange,
Guildhall, Blackwell-hall, at the lord-mayor's door in
St. Helens, at Bow church, and at the western end of
St. Paul's cathedral.—These fires continued for three
days—and were then almost extinguished by a smart
rain; but the following night, from whatever cause it
might proceed, was the most fatal of the whole; for
more than 4000 then expired! and this unfortunate e-
vent was a discouragement to any farther attempts of
that nature.

When the disease was at the greatest height, little
regard was had to the giving medical assistance; for
many of the most eminent physicians and surgeons
were already dead: and it was in vain to keep houses

shut up, when they were mostly empty with their doors and windows open and shattering with the wind. At length the disorder, after having braved the art of man, gave way to the course of nature, at the decline of the summer season, when, though the numbers of the infected were not observed to lessen, yet the disorder grew weaker; more in proportion recovered, and the deaths insensibly diminished. When this began to be perceived, the dread that had invaded the minds of the people wore off, and contributed to their recovery; and whereas in the height of the disorder it usually killed persons in two or three days, and not above one in five recovered—now it did not kill in less than eight or ten days, and not above two in five perished; the nurses also grew either more cautious or more faithful; so that after a little while a dawn of health appeared as suddenly as it was unexpected. In the beginning of November, the face of affairs was quite altered: though the funerals were yet frequent, yet the citizens began to return without fear; and in December they crouded back as fast as they had fled in the spring. Such as were cautious, took great care in seasoning their houses; and abundance of costly things were consumed, which not only answered their own particular purposes, but filled the air with grateful smells, which were serviceable to their neighbours; some burnt pitch, brimstone, and gunpowder, to purge their houses and goods; while others, through eagerness and carelessness, entered their dwellings without any preparation. Earl Craven and the other justices of Westminster caused the bedding of infected houses, to be well dried and aired, the rooms to be new whitewashed, and the churchyards to be covered two feet thick with fresh earth; to prevent, as far as possible, any revival of the pestilential taint.

The winter gave the most effectual check toward suppressing this great enemy of mankind; and tho' some remains of the contagion appeared in the succeeding spring, it was no more than could be easily conquered by medicine; and the city thus got rid of the infection and returned to perfect health.

The bills of mortality computed the numbers of buri-

.als this year at 97,306, of which 68,596 were attributed to the plague; but this eftimate was univerfally received as very erroneous; as it was not difficult to fhow, from circumftances, that the account was manifeftly defective. At the beginning of the diforder, there was great knavery and collufion in the reports of the deaths; for while it was poffible to conceal the infection, they were attributed to fevers of all kinds, which began to fwell the bills; this was done to prevent houfes being fhut up, and families being fhunned by their neighbours. Add to this, that the dead carts working in the dark, no exact accounts were kept; the clerks and fextons being naturally averfe to fo dangerous a duty, and frequently falling fick themfelves before fuch accounts as they had were delivered in. Quakers and Jews alfo; who had feparate burial grounds, were not mentioned in the weekly bills; nor was any regifter taken of thofe who died on board veffels of all kinds in the river. It was well known, that numbers of poor defpairing creatures wandered out of town into the fields, woods, and other remote places, where they died of the infection and of want. The inhabitants of the villages would carry food to thefe diftracted refugees, and fet it at a diftance for them; and afterwards frequently found them dead with the victuals untouched. The country people would then dig holes and drag the bodies into them with long poles having hooks at the ends, carefully ftanding to the windward; and throw the earth over them as far as they could caft it. On the whole, it was the opinion of eye witneffes, that the plague deftroyed 100,000 at leaft. The yearly bill mentions but one parifh that remained quite exempt from infection, which was that of St. John the Evangelift in Watling-ftreet.

As to foreign trade during this year, it was almoft extinct; as no port in France, Flanders, Spain, or Italy, would admit London fhips, or correfpond with that city; the Turks only and the Grecian ifles, to whom the plague was familiar, were not fo fcrupulous. The Flemings and Dutch had great advantage of this circumftance, by buying Englifh goods in thofe parts of England that remained clear of infection, carrying them home, and then exporting them again as their own.

O

MARSEILLES has been several times visited by the plague, as in the year 1580, in 1630, 1649, and 1650.

In May, 1720, the citizens were informed, that the plague had made its appearance in Palestine, and Syria. On the 25th of that month, a vessel from Syria, and the island of Cyprus where the plague prevailed, arrived at the isles of Chateaudif, in the vicinity of the harbour of Marseilles. After performing a quarantine, the passengers were permitted to mix with the inhabitants. One of the crew, and a person placed on board as a guard, had in the mean time died; but the surgeon employed to examine the bodies, declared, that he could discover no mark of the plague. On the 12th of June, a ship, with a foul bill of health, as it is termed, cast anchor. On the 24th and 26th of June, four persons died. Three of these were porters, who had been entrusted with the care of purifying the merchandize on board of these vessels. The fourth was a boy belonging to the first vessel. Hence it appears that the progress of this contagion was in the beginning extremely slow. The surgeon again certified that there was no sign of the plague; but the magistrates began to distrust him. They caused the bodies to be buried in quick lime, and the vessels, from the cargoes of which the porters were suspected of having caught the contagion, were ordered to be removed to a greater distance. On the 7th of July, two other porters employed in the Lazeretto were taken ill, and on the 8th a third; on the 9th, the whole three expired. They were buried in quick lime, and their clothes were burned. Three other surgeons had been appointed to inspect their bodies; and it was at last confessed that they had died of the plague: from this time to the 31st of July, the contagion made feeble but gradual advances. The gentlemen of the faculty, who had declared the dangerous nature of the disease, were insulted by the rabble, who would not believe that the plague would have advanced so very slowly. The magistrates were afraid to injure the commerce of the city by the report spread that this infection had got into

Marfeilles. Though they feem to have done their duty, yet they were fo little aware of the gulf, which was yawning beneath them, that on the 15th of July, they fent letters to the health officers in the other ports of Europe, informing them, that though many perfons were fick in the infirmaries, yet that the contagion had made no progrefs in the city. Indeed, from this day to the 26th, almoft nothing was heard of it, and the people had begun to believe, that the danger was over. On the 26th, however, the magiftrates were informed, that fifteen perfons were taken ill, in the ftreet of Lefcalle. The phyficians durft not venture to declare the fact, and affigned any other reafon for their ficknefs, than the plague.

At the end of July, the magiftrates became alarmed in earneft. Some of them began to be exhaufted by the melancholy employment of attending the funerals of the dead, and the removals of the fick to the public hofpitals, both which offices were performed in the night. The marquis de Pelles, governor of the city, examined the treafury, and found in it only the pitiful fum of eleven hundred livres. Corn, butcher's meat, and wood, were extremely fcarce and dear. The wealthy part of the inhabitants had by this time fled. It was now certain that the contagion was fixed in the city; and it was readily forefeen, that, unlefs vigorous meafures of prevention were taken, famine would complete the fcene of calamity. All beggars from the country were commanded to leave the city; but it was immediately found impracticable, to carry this order into execution. The chamber of trade of the parliament of Aix, had publifhed an arret, prohibiting the citizens of Marfeilles from quitting the territories of the town, The other inhabitants of Provence were forbidden to hold any correfpondence with them; and coachmen, carriers, or others, attempting to retire from Marfeilles to the country, on any pretence whatever, were to return back under pain of death. It was, therefore, impoffible to drive out of the city, two or three thoufand beggars, and other ftrangers of different kinds. An attempt was made to difpel the infection by burning fire in the ftreets, but to no purpofe. A variety of regulations were adopted to prevent the fpreading of the diftemper, as well as the progrefs of famine. What fuel had been in the city, was already confumed in the experiment of making fires. A great quantity of fulphur was bought, and a part of it diftributed to the poor, in every quarter of the town, to be burned in their houfes by way of a perfume; the colleges and fchools were fhut up, to prevent the communication of the diforder; and the moft preffing applications were made to the government of France, for immediate and fubftantial affiftance, before the avenues of the city fhould be abfolutely fhut up. On the third of Auguft, a mob affembled, demanding bread, which was given to them. On the fourth, the officers of the fort of St. John, waited on the magiftrates, to acquaint them, that their foldiers were in want of corn; and if not fupplied, would perhaps enter the city, and take it by force; the anfwer which they received was, that if the troops attempted to enter Marfeilles, the magiftrates, at the head of the citizens, would oppofe them. On the 7th of Auguft, the chamber of trade of Provence, permitted the fheriffs to have a conference with fome of their agents, at the diftance of fix miles from the city. Precautions were taken to fpeak at a diftance. An agreement was made, that a market fhould be eftablifhed in that place, and a double barrier erected. Another market was to be fixed upon a high road, two leagues from Marfeilles, in a different direction. A rendezvous for boats was likewife named, in a creek amongft the iflands in the harbour of Marfeilles. In all thefe places, the guards were appointed by the province, and paid by the city. On the 9th of Auguft, it was found, that moft of the phyficians and furgeons had fled. It was thought neceffary to felect a houfe to which the fick might be carried. The houfe of convalefcence was pitched upon for that purpofe. But it was an object of the greateft difficulty to remove the fick. Horfes, harnefs, and carts were all equally wanted. It became neceffary to go into the country to feek them, and when they were found, no perfon would confent to ferve as a porter in removing the dead—Exorbitant wages were offered with little effect. An immenfe number of cooks and fick nurfes were likewife wanted, and it was not without the greateft exertions, that the ma-

giftrates could obtain perfons for thefe employments.
Three pits were dug without the walls of the city.
They were fixty feet in length and twenty four feet
deep, and the dead were buried in quick lime. Another large hofpital was fitted up under the vaults of a
rope yard, by the chevalier Rofe, at his own expenfe;
and he caufed large ditches to be dug for burying the
dead. The two hofpitals were entirely filled in lefs than
two days; but the patients did not remain there long.
The diftemper was fo violent, that thofe who were
brought into the hofpitals at night, were caft into the
ditches next morning. In every houfe where it entered,
no perfon efcaped the infection, and it feems that few or
none furvived it. On the 12th of Auguft, two of the
moft eminent phyficians of Montpelier were difpatched
by the regent of France to the affiftance of the citizens.
The magiftrates of health, the judges of the city, the
rectors of all the hofpitals and other charitable founda-
tions, the commiffaries who had been appointed for the
different quarters of the city, but a few days before,
with an immenfe number of people of all ranks, fled in
the greateft hurry from Marfeilles. The very centinels
who had been pofted to prevent the flight of others,
deferted, while the captains of the militia, and their
foldiers ran away by whole companies. The fhops,
houfes, magazines, churches and convents were fhut up.
The public markets were empty, and nothing was any
where to be feen, but the dying or the dead. Marfeilles was fuppofed at this time to contain about one
hundred thoufand people. Carts and porters were kept
in conftant readinefs to carry off the dead; but the difficulty of providing thefe augmented every day. Perfons employed in that fervice very feldom lived more
than forty eight hours. It is faid that by only touching
the body with an iron hook, at the end of a pole, the
diftemper was communicated. Fifteen livres or
about three dollars per day was the hire offered,
and it was refufed by the very beggars. At laft, the magiftrates applied to the officers of the gallies, and obtained from them a fupply of hands, felected from the
criminals, who were promifed their pardon upon condition of exerting themfelves; but they did their work

with so much flowness and lazineſs, ſays our author, *that it was enough to make one mad.* The ſlaves were in want of every thing, and in particular of ſhoes, which it was impoſſible to get for them, as there was none in the city, nor any ſhoemaker, to manufacture them. Theſe unfortunate beings, when they entered a houſe, to carry off the dead, hardly ever failed to plunder it, ſo that the perpetual danger of robbery was added to the other calamities of the citizens. The ſlaves were likewiſe unſkilful as well as unwilling carters. They frequently overturned the carts, and broke the harneſs of the horſes; a loſs which was irreparable, for neither ſaddler nor cartwright was left in Marſeilles. Beſides, no tradeſman would touch the carts or harneſs which were employed in that ſervice; and the peaſants in the territory belonging to the city, had carefully concealed their carts.

Multitudes of women, who were giving ſuck, died of the plague; and their infants were found ſome dead; and others dying in the cradles. An hoſpital and a convent, which were found empty, by the death or flight of their former poſſeſſors, ſerved as an aſylum for theſe noviciates in wretchedneſs. They were ſupplied with ſoup, and goats milk. Thirty or forty of them periſhed every day; yet there were never leſs than twelve or thirteen hundred of them ſurviving at one time. On the 21ſt of Auguſt, the number of the dead at once increaſed ſo prodigiouſly, that the magiſtrates found it impracticable to get them carried out of town, to be thrown into the pits. The quarter of St. John and ſome other parts of the old town, were, from the height of the ground and the narrowneſs of the ſtreets, almoſt inacceſſible to any wheel carriage. They were inhabited by the pooreſt claſſes of the people, who were worſt lodged and worſt fed, and therefore died faſteſt. The bodies, in heaps, blocked up the paſſages of the ſtreets. It was to be apprehended, that if they were ſuffered to lie above ground, the infection would ſpread with augmented rapidity. The marquis de Pille and the magiſtrates, requeſted a meeting at the town houſe, with the officers of the gallies. This aſſembly came to the reſolution of interring the dead bodies, belonging to the

higher parts of the town, in the vaults of the church
yards in the neighbourhood. Quick lime and water
were to be thrown upon them, and the vaults, when
full, were to be closely cemented up. The bishop of
Marseilles and the clergy opposed this measure; but
the necessity of the case superceded every objection. On
the 23d of August the magistrates began this task. The
clergy had bolted the doors of their churches, which
were broke open. In the mean time, the misery of the
inhabitants augmented every day and almost every hour.
Amongst other necessaries, linen was exhausted, and in
the midst of this mass of wretchedness, the populace,
from famine, despair, and madness, had become so
turbulent, that it was found requisite to raise gibbets in
all the public places of the city. From the 25th of August to the end of September, a thousand persons were
computed to perish every day. The galley slaves, who
had been called to assist the citizens, began to die like
the rest. The shopkeepers had locked up their doors,
so that the people could not buy, on any terms, the
common necessaries of life. On the 27th, the board of
trade published an order, for all shopkeepers and tradesmen, to set open their doors, within twenty-four hours,
on the pain of death. Commands of this kind had little
weight. Desertion, wherever it could be accomplished,
was universal.

On whatever side the spectator cast his eye, nothing
was to be seen but heaps of putrefaction. The streets,
the public markets, the square of the play house, the
harbour, and every other place, was strewed with dead
bodies. In the original narrative, from which this abridg-
ment is extracted, there are many circumstances related,
of a nature so shocking, that to repeat them would be
an act of inhumanity to the reader. Thousands fled on
board the ships in the harbour, from a conceit, which
proved very foolish, that the contagion could not reach
them, when upon the water. The streets were heaped
not only with dead bodies, but with furniture and
clothes of persons infected, which were incessantly cast
out of the windows. The dogs and cats were every
where killed, and served to augment the mass of corrup-

tion. Ten thousand dogs were at one time computed to be floating in the harbour.

If you met any one in the streets, he looked as if half dead, and as if the distemper had affected his understanding. Many wandering about fell through weakness, and never rose again. Some, to put an end to their sufferings, cut their own throats, or jumped out of high windows, or into the sea. It was impossible for the hospitals to contain the crouds of patients who thronged into them. The instant that a person was observed to be infected, he became an object of horror to his nearest relations. He was either left deserted in the house, or driven out of it. This was the treatment of wives to their husbands, and husbands to their wives, of children to their parents, and of parents to their children. The hospitals were so far from being capable to contain the sick, that numbers could not even get access to the doors, on account of the vast crouds that lay on the pavement around them. This was the situation of Marseilles at the end of August. By the third of September, the surviving magistrates found the town house almost empty. Five hundred persons belonging to it had died. Amongst these were three hundred and fifty of the city guards. The religious orders likewise suffered extremely. The bishop was distinguished by the most active and intrepid benevolence. On the 6th of September, there remained, after every exertion, above two thousand dead bodies in the streets. A fresh supply of galley slaves was obtained with difficulty. From this time, to the end of September, the disease raged with unabated fury. In the month of October, it began to abate without any visible cause. The sick began to be cured. In November, the contagion continued to decrease, and by the 1st of December, the danger was in a great measure at an end. It was not, however, entirely ceased till the month of March. We are not informed as to the exact number of deaths; but they are estimated at not less than fifty or sixty thousand.

Lift of all the Burials in the feveral grave yards of the city and liberties of Philadelphia, as taken from the Books kept by Clergymen, Sextons, &c. from August 1ft to November 9th, 1793.

AUGUST.

DAYS.	Christ Church.	St. Peter's.	St. Paul's.	First Presbyterian.	Second Presbyterian.	Third Presbyterian.	Scotch Presbyterian.	Seceders.	St. Mary's.	Trinity.	Friends.	Free Quakers.	German Lutherans.	German Calvinifts.	Moravians.	Swedes.	Baptifts.	Methodifts.	Univerfalifts.	Jews,	Kenfington.	Potter's field.	Total.
1	1	2		1	2					1			1			1							9
2					1	1			2					1		2					2	1	8
3		1			1	1			2	2						2					1		9
4	1			1		1	1		1	2		4									5	2	10
5	1												1										10
6	1												2										3
7	1		1							7											2		12
8				1					1				1	1							1	1	5
9	2			1	1	1				2			2	2							1	1	11
10	1	1			1								4								1	1	6
11						2															1		7
12					1				2	2			2		*Returned in grofs.*	1	*Returned in grofs.*	*Returned in grofs.*	*Returned in grofs.*		1		5
13				1					2	1			2	1		1					1	2	11
14					1								2	1							1	2	4
15									3				2	1							2	2	9
16		1	1										1	1							2	1	7
17				1							1		1								2	1	6
18											1		1										5
19			1	1		1			1	3			1								1		9
20	1		1	1					3	1				1							1		7
21	2			1					2		1		1									2	8
22			1		2				4		3		1									1	13
23		1							2	1			3	1								3	10
24				3	1	1		1	2		1		3							1	1	1	17
25	1				2	1			2		1		3							2	1	1	12
26	2	2			1				3		1		4	1						1	1	1	17
27	1	1		2					2				3				1					2	12
28	5	3			1	2			3		1		2	3								3	22
29	4	2	1			2	2		2	1	3		4								1	3	24
30	1	1							4		4		3	3								3	20
31	2	1							3				7									3	17

P

DAYS.	Christ Church.	St. Peter's	St. Pauls.	First Presbyterian.	Second Presbyterian.	Third Presbyterian.	Associate Presb.	Reformed.	St. Mary's.	Trinity.	Friends.	Free Quakers.	German Lutherans.	German Calvinists.	Moravians.	Swedes.	Baptists.	Methodists.	Universalists.	Jews.	Kensington.	Potter's field.	Total.
1	1				2	1		1					4			1					2	5	17
2					2				2	5			3	1							1	4	18
3	1	1			3	1							2									3	11
4	3		1	1	2				2	1			4	3							2	2	23
5		4		1	1		1	1					2	3							1	5	20
6		2		1	2				2	1			5	1							2	7	24
7	1			1	1	4			1	1			3								1	7	18
8	2	1		1	4	2			2				4	4		2					1	16	42
9		1	2		4	1			1	3			7	1	1						1	13	32
10	3		1	1	1				2	3	1	6	5	1							4	8	29
11	2	1			1			1	2	2			5			1					3	8	23
12	1	2	6		1	1			2	3			2	2	1	1					2	10	33
13	1	1			1	1			3	1	7		8	2		1					1	10	37
14	2	1	2	3	3	1			4	4	4		5	2							2	15	48
15	4	2		1	1	3	1		5	1	10		9	1	1	1					2	14	56
16	4	2	1	2	3	1			4	3	10		12	7		1					3	14	57
17	1	1	1	1	4	2			5	2	7		21	7							3	20	81
18	3	4		2	4				6	2	7		10	4		2					2	23	68
19	4	2		2	3	2			6	4			9	5							2	23	61
20	3	1	1	1	2	2		2	3	5	9		7	5		3					5	27	57
21	3	3			1	2	1		6	6			8	2							4	21	57
22	6	1		2	3	1	1		1	6			7	6	1	1					7	33	76
23	1	3	2		4				5	2	7		8	6							9	21	58
24		5	2	4	4	2			9		8		12	4							8	38	96
25	4	2		1	4			2	6		5		15	5		3					7	25	87
26	2		1	3					1	1	5		6	5		1					2	14	60
27	3	1	1	2	1	4	1		6		14		6	5							2	29	60
28	1	1	1	1	1	1				2			4	5		3					2	29	51
29	4		3	2	2	3		1	4	1	10		7	3		1					2	14	57
30	4	1	2	1	3				6	1	8		4	6		3					2	22	3L

Free Quakers — Returned in gross.
Baptists — Returned in gross.
Universalists — Returned in gross.
Jews — Returned in gross.

DAYS.	Christ Church.	St. Peter's.	St. Paul's.	First Presbyterian.	Second Presbyterian.	Third Presbyterian.	Associate Presb.	Reformed.	St. Mary's.	Trinity.	Friends.	Free Quakers.	German Lutherans.	German Calvinists.	Moravians.	Swedes.	Baptists.	Methodists.	Universalists.	Jews.	Kensington.	Potter's field.	Total.
1	4	2	5	1	3	4			4	·	8		12			2				5		21	74
2	2	1	1	3	1	2		2	3	1	9	*Returned in grofs.*	5	5								31	67
3	3	1	1	3	2	3			5	7			10	4	1						2	33	78
4	1	2	4		2	3		1	3	5	3		6	5		2			1		1	27	58
5		2	1		2	3			3	1	12		11	3	1	4					3	26	71
6	2	5	1	1	3	2	1		5		5		14	4		2						34	76
7	7	3	1	2	1	5	1	2	5	2	9		12	7		2					2	25	82
8	3	2	3	1	2	1		2	3	2	5		21	6		3					3	33	90
9	2	1		2	2	2		1	7	1	6		19	8	1	1	2				3	50	102
10	7		2	2	2	2			3	1	6		26	6	1	2			1		2	31	93
11	4	2	5	1	3	2			3	1	12		21	8		5					2	50	119
12	2	2	2	1	4	1			6	1	11		17	12		1		*Returned in grofs.*			8	44	111
13	6	3			1		1	1	4	1	9		20	5		1				4		48	104
14	2		1		1	5			2	2	5		17	7	1	7				2		29	81
15	3	3	1	1	2	1			4	1	9		14	7		2			*Returned in grofs.*		3	29	80
16	1	1	2	2	4	2		2	3	1	4		16	7		2					2	29	70
17	5	3	2					3	6		10		16	7		2					1	28	80
18		2	1		4		1		5	1	5		11	3	1	1					2	22	59
19	2	3			4	1			4	2	2		14	2	1	1					2	27	65
20	2	3			3	2			4	1	4		11	6		1					1	17	55
21	4			2	3	1			5	2	4		8	4		1					1	24	59
22	2			2	3	2	2		5	2	7		19	7	2	1					2	31	82
23	1			1	3				5	3			10	7							1	3	54
24	1	1				3			2		2		8	4								17	38
25	5			1	2	1	1	1	1	1	1		8	2		1					2	10	35
26	2	1			1	1		1		1	2		5	2	1						1	5	23
27	1		1					1			1		5	2	1							6	13
28	1	1		2							4		5	3							1	6	25
29	1				1				1		2		4	2								6	17
30	1	1							2		1		3	1							2	6	16
31									2		1		7	3								8	22

DAYS.	Christ Church.	St. Peter's.	St. Paul's.	First Presbyterian.	Second Presbyterian.	Third Presbyterian.	Associate Presb.	Reformed	St. Mary's.	Trinity.	Friends.	Free Quakers.	German Lutherans.	German Calvinists.	Moravians.	Swedes.	Baptists.	Methodists.	Universalists.	Jews.	Kensington	Potter's field.	Total.
1									1		3										2	5	13
2		1				2			3		2		1	2								8	21
3	1	1							3		1		3	2							1	4	15
4	1	1							1				5				Returned in gross.	Returned in gross.		Returned in gross.	1	6	15
5	2										3		2	1								6	14
6		1							3		1		1	1								5	11
7	2			1					1		4			1							1	5	15
8		1							2			1		1								3	8
9									1	1					2							3	6

Auguſt	325
September	1442
October	1993
November	118
Jews, returned in groſs	5
Baptiſts, Do.	60
Methodiſts, Do.	32
Free Quakers, Do.	39
German part of St. Mary's congregation	30
	———
Total	4041

Proteſtant Epiſcopalians	Chriſt Church - - -	173
	St. Peter's - - -	109
	St. Paul's. - - -	70
Preſbyterians	Firſt - - - -	73
	Second - - -	128
	Third - - -	107
	Aſſociate - -	12
	Reformed - - -	33
Roman Catholics	St. Mary's - - -	251
	German part of do. - -	30
	Trinity - - -	54
Friends - - - - -		373
Free Quakers - -	Returned in groſs. -	39
German	Lutherans - - -	641
	Calviniſts - - -	261
Moravians - - - - -	r	13
Swedes - - - - -		75
Baptiſts - -	Returned in groſs. -	60
Methodiſts - -	Do. -	32
Univerſaliſts - -		2
Jews - - - -	Do. - -	2
Kenſington - - -		169
Potter's field, including the new ground - -		1334
		————
		4041

Q

METEOROLOGICAL OBSER

MADE IN PHILADELPHIA,

DAVID RITTENHOUSE,

AUGUST, 1793.

	Barometer.				Thermometer.		Wind.	
	A. M.		3 P. M.		6 A. M.	3 P. M.	6 A. M.	3 P. M.
1	29	95	30	0	65	77	WNW	NW
2	30	1	30	1	63	81	NW	SW
3	30	5	29	95	64	82	N	NNE
4	29	97	30	0	65	87	S	SW
5	30	5	30	1	73	90	SSW	SW
6	30	2	30	0	77	87	SW	W
7	30	12	30	1	68	83	NW	W
8	30	1	29	95	69	86	SSE	SSE
9	29	8	29	75	75	85	SSW	SW
10	29	9	29	9	67	82	W	SW
11	30	0	30	0	70	84	SW	WSW
12	30	0	30	0	70	87	W	W
13	30	5	30	0	71	89	SW	W
14	30	0	29	95	75	82	SW	SW
15	30	0	30	1	72	75	NNE	NE
16	30	1	30	1	70	83	NNE	NE
17	30	1	30	0	71	86	SW	SW
18	30	1	30	0	73	89	calm	SW
19	30	1	30	1	72	82	N	N
20	30	1	30	12	69	82	NNE	NNE
21	30	15	30	25	62	83	N	NNE
22	30	3	30	35	63	86	NE	SE
23	30	25	30	15	63	85	calm	S
24	30	1	30	1	73	81	calm	calm
25	30	1	30	1	71	66	NE	NE
26	30	15	30	2	59	69	NE	NE
27	30	2	30	2	65	73	NE	NE
28	30	2	30	15	67	80	S	calm
29	30	16	30	15	72	86	calm	SW
30	30	1	30	1	74	87	calm	SW
31	30	0	30	0	74	84	SW	NW

PHILADELPHIA, SEPTEMBER, 1793.

Barometer.		Thermometer.		Winds.		Weather.	
6 A.M.	3 P.M.	6 A.M.	3 P.M	6 A.M.	3 P.M.	6 A.M.	3 P.M.
30 0	29 30	71	86	Calm'	SW	fog,	fair,
29 75	29 8	73	86	SW	SW	fair,	fair,
80 0		60		NW	N	fair,	fair,
30 ·15	30 15	55	75	W	W	fair,	fair,
30 ·15	30 1	62	80	SE	S	fair,	cloudy,
29 97	29 95	70	89	WSW	W	fair,	cloudy,
30 0	30 0	65	77	WNW	NW	fair,	fair, .
30 1	30 1	64	70	Calm	Calm	cloudy,	cloudy,
30 0·	30 0	66	80	SE	NW	rain,	fair,
30 0	30 0	64	72	N	NNE	fair,	cloudy, .
30 1	30 0	64	72	NE	N	cloudy,	fair,
29 96	29 9	58	76	W	NNW	fair, .	fair,
29 95	30 0	57	72	W	N	fair,	fair,
30 ·0	30 5	58	79	NW	NW	fair,	fair, .
30 0	29 97	65	80	N	S	fair,	fair,
29 9	29	70	84	S	SW	cloudy,	fair,
29 8	29 85	66	67	N	N	cloudy,	cloudy,
30 3		44		N		fair,	
30 4	30 35	45	70	Calm	SW	fair,	fair,
30 3	30 15	54	69	Calm	SE	hazey,	hazey,
30 0	29 0	59	78	Calm		cloudy,	fair,
30 0.	30 0	63	83	Calm		cloudy,	fair,
30 1	30 1	62	81	Calm	SE	cloudy,	cloudy,
30 ·2	30 2	65	70	NE	ENE	cloudy,	fair,
30 15	30 0	61	68	NE	NE	cloudy,	cloudy,
29 8	29 7	58	79	N	N	cloudy,	fair.
29 7		64		NW	NW	cloudy,	fair,
30 5	30 15	54	73	NW	NW	fair,	fair,
30 3	30 3	56	74	NE	ENE	cloudy,	fair,
30 35	30 3	57	73	Calm	SW	foggy,	fair,

METEOROLOGICAL OBSERVATION

PHILADELPHIA, OCTOBER, 1793.

	Barometer.		Thermometer.		Winds.		Weather	
	7 A.M.	2 P.M.	7 A.M.	2 P.M.	7 A.M.	2 P.M.	7 A.M.	2 P.
1	30 15	30 5	64	80	SW	SW	cloudy,	fai
2	29 9	30 5	70	72	W	NNW	cloudy,	fai
3	30 2	30 15	50	72	W	SW	fair,	fai
4	29 75	29 7	59	72	SW	W	cloudy,	clo
5	30 0	30 1	58	66	N	N	fair,	fai
6	30 3	30 3	43	66	NE	W	fair,	fai
7	30 45		46		calm		fair,	
8	30 6	30 6	53	68	N	N	fair,	fai
9	30 5	30 4	53	70	NW	NW	fair,	fai
10	30 2	30 2	49	74	E	NW	fair,	fai
11	30 0	29 85	51	74	W	W	fair,	fai
12	26 6	29 55	58	64	SW	NW	rain,	rai
13	29 85	29 0	49	69	NW	NW	fair,	fai
14	30 5	30 0	52	76	SW	SW	calm,	fai
15	29 75	29 8	56	54	SW	N	fair,	rai
16	30 0	30 0	37	53	NNW	N	fair,	fai
17	30 1	30 1	37	60	NE	NE	fair,	fai
18	30 1	30 1	41	62	NW	NW	fair,	fai
19	30 0	29 9	51	66	N	N	cloudy,	fai
20	30 0	30 0	44	54	NW	N	fair,	fai
21	30 0	30 2	49	59	N	NW	fair,	fai
22	29 6	29 5	51	65	NW	NW	fair,	fai
23	29 8	29 8	47	6c	W	W	fair,	fai
24	30 3	30 4	36	59	W	NW	fair,	fat
25	30 4	30 3	46	71	S	S	cloudy, fair,b	
26	30 2	30 2	60	72	calm	SW	cloudy,	clo
27	30 3	30 3	44	44	NNE	NNE	cloudy,	clo
28	30 2	30 1	34	37	N	N	cloudy,	clo
29	29 85	29 85	28	44	NNW	NW	fair,	fa
30	30 1	30 1	28	49	calm	SW	hazy,	ha
31	30 15	30 2	42	45	calm	NNE	cloudy,	ra

NOVEMBER, 1793.

	Barometer.		Thermometer.		Wind.		Weather	
	7 A.M.	2 P.M.	7 A.M.	2 P.M.	7 A.M.	2 P.M.	7 A.M.	2 P.
1	30 1	30 1	40	41	NNE	NE	rain,	clo
2	30 3	30 25	32	49	NNE	NE	fair,	fair
3	30 1	30 0	43	56	Calm	SW	cloudy,	clo
4	29 8	29 9	55	67	SW	SW	cloudy,	fai
5	30 15	30 1	50	64	NE	NE	rain,	ra
6	29 8	29 65	63	67	S	S	cloudy,	clo
7	29 8	29 8	44	64	Calm	SW	fair,	fai
8	29 8	29 85	43	56	SSW	SW	fair,	fai
9	29 9	29 95	42	64	SW	SW	fair,	fai

LIST of the names of the perfons who died in Philadelphia, or in different parts of the union, after their departure from this city, from Auguft 1ft, to the middle of December, 1793*.

ABIGAIL, a negrefs
    Jofeph Abbot
John Abel, fhoemaker
Henry Abel's child
John Abrahams, fhopkeeper
Elizabeth Abraham
James Ackley, labourer, wife, and three daughters
John B. Ackley's child
Widow Ackley
James Adair, labourer, wife, and fon
Hefter Adams
Mofes Adams, carpenter
Robert Adams's two children
Sarah Adams, fervant girl
Andrew Adgate, cardmaker
Widow Adgate and 2 children
Mary Addington
James Ager
Peter Agge, phyfician
Mary Advulter
John Ainey, ftone-cutter
John Alberger, cooper
Chriftian Alberger, fkinner
Jofeph Alberton, wife, and two children
Wife of Tho's Alberton, farmer
Frederic Albrecht
————Albrecht, fkinner
Michael Albrecht's fon Michael
————Antonio, clerk, Portugal
Andrew Apple, and child
Henry Apple, tailor
Elizabeth Appleby, fervant girl
Henry Apfel's daughter
Benjamin Armand and child
Chriftopher Arpurth's wife
Andrew Armftrong's child
Barney Armftrong, labourer
Chriftian Armftrong, weaver
Hugh Armftrong, weaver

Chriftopher Armftong, weaver
James Armftrong, weaver
John Armftrong
Michael Artery
John Afh, breeches-maker
George Afhen
Nathaniel Afhby's child
John Afhton, labourer, and wife
Jofeph Afhton, bricklayer, wife and two children
Jofeph Afhton, carpenter
Jofeph Afhtin
Stephen Afton, labourer
Kitty Auftin, feamftrefs
Peter Afton, merchant, wife, and fon
John Atkinfon
Caleb Attmore, hatter and his apprentice
Jane Attrictz, wid. & daughter
James Aubaine
Phil B. Audibert, merchant, Fr.
Monfieur Anje, Fr.
Julia Aulet, fervant girl
Ifaac Auftin, cnrrier
Remiquis Azor
Prifcilla Alberton
James Alder, merchant
Thomas Allibone's child
Elifha Alexander, tailor
James Alexander, hatter
Jofeph Alexander, weaver, & apprentice
———— Alexander's wife, & an apprentice
Hefter Alexander
Rebecca Alexander
Nicholas Allaway, labourer
Auguftus Allbrink, and 3 chil.
Elizabeth Allegue
Ann Allen
James Allen's child

* This lift has been partly collected from the church-hooks of all the different congregations, and partly from the information received by feveral perfons who have been employed to make enquiry at every houfe in the city and liberties. Though very great pains have been taken, and expenfe incurred, in its arrangement, ftill it is not given as fully complete and accurate. But, it is hoped, that its defects and errors are but few, and, confidering the difficulty of the bufinefs, fuch only, as will meet the reader's ready indulgence. R

John Allen, foap boiler
Mary Allen, aged 70
Joseph Allen
Mary Allen
Widow Rebecca Allen
David Allen's fifter
William Allen, fervant
William Alley
George Allifon, fadler
Robert Allifon, fen.
Lawrence Allman and child
John Allman
Jacob Aloerftock, brewer
John Alton, medical ftndent
Peter Alyart
Sarah Ammond
————, Amand
Francis Anderfon
Francis Anderfon's child
Alexander Anderfon, innkeeper
Hugh Anderfon, tailor
James Anderfon's wife
Sufanna Anders
William Anderfon, aged 72
Jacob Anderfon's daughter
John Andre'
Thomas Andrews, fhoemaker,
  and fon
Ifaac Andrews
Rev. Robert Annan's wife
Jacob Anthony's wife, and fon
  Henry
Thomas P. Anthony, merchant
Michael Babb
John Bacon's wife
David Bacon's wife
Mary Bacon
Widow Backer
Elizabeth Back
George Backley
John Badley, farmer
Jacob Baden, labourer
Hugh Bain's child
Mrs. Bakeoven, tavern-keeper
Adam Baker
Samuel Baker, bookbinder
Bartholomew Baker's child
Catharine Baker
Chriftiana Baker, widow
George Baker, merchant
Jane Baker, widow
Michael Baker, fhoemaker
Sarah Baker
Wallace Baker

William Baker, fen.
Wm. Baker, jun. apprentice
George Baldy, tanner
Daniel Baldwin, apothecary
Burgefs Ball
Henry Ball, or Bale, fadler
Hannah Bales
John Ballance, blackfmith
Thomas Ballentine
Dougal Ballentine
James Balling, gunfmith
John Balluftree's child
Mary Banks
Jacob Bankfon's widow & child
George Bantteon's child
John Bap.ifte
Barbara ————, a fervant
Barbe, a black woman
John Barber, carpenter
Ifaac Barber, plafterer
Jacob Barkelow's child
John Barkley's child
Mary Barclay and child
Ifrael Bard
Thomas Barker, chair-maker
John Barker
Wade Barker, an apprentice
Mary Bare
Margaret Barkett
Blair Barnes, hair-dreffer
Cornelius Barnes, merchant
Steiman Barnes, merchant
Francis Barnes
Paul Barnes's fon
Ifaac Barnett, joiner
Garret Barrey, type-founder
John Barret's child
James Barrett's wife
Bridget Barret
Edward Barrington, grocer
James Barry and child
Matthias Barry
Peter Bartbo, apprentice
Peter Barthol, cooper, and wife
———— Bartholomew, failor
Elizabeth Bartholomew
Charles Bartholomew's wife
Chriftlieb Bartling's wife & dau.
———— Barren
Alexander Barron, labourer
Lewis Barron
Thomas Barry
William, fon of John Barry
Robert Bartram, fon of Jofeph

John Barwell, livery-stable-
  keeper, and wife
John Bass, apprentice
Francis Baftian
Magdalen Baftian
Lawrence Baft, labourer
William Baftin's son
Abraham Bates
Peter Batto, cooper
Catharine, widow of Tho's Batt
Widow Batt's daughter
Sufan Batty
John Batty
John Baufh, fhoemaker
Anna Barbara Bauer
Catharine Bauchman
Elizabeth Bauck, a fervant
Peter Baufan's son
Henry Charles Bauman, weaver
Andrew Baufh
Adam Baufh, reed-maker
George Bautz, carter
Charles Bayman, wheelwright
Jacob Bay, type-founder
Elizabeth Bayle
James Beak, labourer
Honour Beale
Nathaniel Baine's wife
William Beard, blackfmith
Bridget Bearet
John Bear's wife
John Beattie, labourer, & wife
John Beattie, porter of united
  ftates bank
Catharine Beattie
Elizabeth Beaufort
Charles Beaumont
Andrew Beck, fen. dyer
Andrew Beck, jun.
Eliza. daugh. of Andrew Beck
Bernard Beck, porter
Catharine Beck
Jacob Beck's wife and daughter
Almy Beck
John Beck, fen. dyer
John Beck, jun.
Eliza. daughter of John Beck
Peter Beck, fhoemaker
Mary Beckener
Rachel Beck
George Becker's child
Jacob Beeker
Margaret Beeves

———— Beifs, labourer
Alexander Beicht's child
Elizabeth Bell
John Bell
Maria Antoniette Belvoire
Catharine Benard
Elizabeth Benge
Francis Benjie
John Bennet, joiner, and wife
Samuel Bennet
Michael Benner, labourer
Jacob Benner
Benjamin Benoit's child
Thomas Bennet, labourer
Lucy Bennet, wife of ditto
Ofwald Bently
John Benfon's child
Rene Berenger, Fr.
Margaret Bergmeyer
Mary Berg, Æt. 75
———— Berry, tinker, and wife
Catharine Berry's child
Colonel William Berry
Nicholas Berkelet
Daniel Befkmeyer
Claudius A. Bertier, merchant
Henry Beyer
Samuel Bettle, fen. tailor
George Betinger
Abraham Betts
John Betz
Peter Betto
Thomas Bevans
Mary Bevans
Chriftopher Bevelin, labourer
Jenny Bickledick
Ann Bickley
Margaret Bideman
Owen Biddle's daughter Jane
Henry Pierfe, fhoemaker
John Biggs, linen-draper, and
  wife
Eleanor Bigley
Peter Bignall's wife
Ann Bigot
Jacob Binder
Jacob Bilerder's child
Anna Bird, fervant
Francis Bingin
Cornelius Bird
Jofeph Bird's child
Chriftopher Birger, carter
Thomas Birmingham

Ann Birmingham
Ann Bishop
Thomas Bishop's daughter
Thomas Biven
John Peter Bittman
Robert Black, bricklayer
William Blake's child
Anthony Blame, confectioner
Widow Blofbeyer
Nathaniel Blodget, Virginia planter
Stancy Blockler
Jacob Blocher, labourer
Jacob Blocher, shoemaker
Jacob Blocker's wife
—— Blofbeyer's grandchild
Elizabeth Bliney
Eliza Blackley
Robert Black ·
Rich. Blackham, ironmonger
Bernard Bravehoufe
Charles Boehm, apprentice
Charlotte Boehm, a fervant
Adam Bohl, carpenter, and two daughters
Martha Boggs, widow
Thomas Bogh, shoemaker
—— Bogs
George Bounce, carter
George Bock's fifter
Widow Bock
Mary Bock
Margaret Bond, fpinfter
Peter Bob's daughter
Widow Bohn's fon
Joshua Bonn, carpenter
Henry Bonn, labourer
Jemimah Bonfhall
Sarah Bonnel, a child
Sarah Bird
Barney Book, and child
Thomas Boone, carpenter
Joseph Borde, fawyer
Geo. Bornhoufe, cabinet-maker
John Bafs's wife
Benjamin James Boflock
Andreas Bofhart, shoemaker, wife and fon
Wife of Andrew Bofhart, fen.
Wife of Wm. Bofton, baker
Elizabeth Bofwell
Jemimah Bofwell
Charlotte Bower

Widow Boulter
Saliniah Bouman
Catharine Bourke
Peter Bourke, hatter
Andrew Bower's wife
Martha Bowers
Stephen Bowers, shoemaker
Mrs. Bowen
Joseph Bowen
Elizabeth Bowen
Adam Bowles, carpenter
Catharine Bowles
Henry Bowles's wife and 2 fons
Sufannah Bowles
Catharine Bowman, a fervant
James Bowman
Frederic Bowman, doorkeeper
Frederic Bowman
Henry Bower's wife
John Bowyer, gardener
William Boyce's wife and fon
Elizabeth Boyd
Martha Boyd, fervant
Anthony Boyer, ftore-keeper
Catharine Boyer, widow
Henry Boyer, coachmaker
Michael Boyer's child
Michael Boyer, butcher
James Boylan's child
Mary Boyles, widow
Catharine Boynes
Benjamin Bodger's fon
Mary Brackley, a fervant
Ann Bradfhaw
Riley Bradford, waterman
Mr. Brandhoffer
John Brailey
Jacob Brant, blackfmith
John Braun's wife
Martin Braun, labourer
Widow Brayton's two children
Francis A. Breinez
Michael Brady
John Brady
William Brickhoufe
Hugh Barnes's child
Charles Brinhon
Mary Brady
Paul Breckel's wife
Therefa Briftol
Anthony Bricour
Catharine Breflin
Michael Briefch, tailor

Eliza Brelew
Rose Bride
Joseph Brewer, merchant
Samuel Breslin
John Bretzel, baker
William Brewster's son
Christian Bridig
Samuel Brien's daughter
Catharine Britton
Isaac Britton
Peter Bridnen, labourer
John Bright's son
Sarah Bright
Francis Brooks, gunsmith, and child
Jacob Broener, tailor, and wife
Edward Brookes's wife
William Brookes's daughter
Mary Brooks
Francis Brookes
Wife of ——— Brooks, invalid
Hannah Brooks
— Broomstone & 2 apprentices
Widow Elizabeth Brogdon
John Brother's apprentice
John Brown, a negro
Ann Brown
Mary Brown
Barbara Brown, a servant
Conrad Brown and wife
Wife of George Brown, tailor
F. Brown, tailor, and wife
Jacob Brown, jun.
John Brown, carpenter
John Brown, brickmaker
Martin Brown and mother
Thomas Brown, tailor
William Brown, labourer
Thomas Brown, shopman
Thomas Brown, labourer
James Brown
Elizabeth Brown
William Brown
George Brownpere, labourer
Francis Bruckner
Barnabas Bruckholst and wife
James Broadwick
John Brunstrom
George Bruner, tailor, & wife
Widow Bruner
Elizabeth Bryant
Jacob Bryant, blacksmith
John Bryan's wife and child

Matthew Bryan, tailor
Peter Bryan, shoemaker
Thomas A. Bryan
Thomas Bryan's wife
William Bryan, labourer
Isaac Buckbee, hatter
George Buck, baker
Bernard Buck's daughter
Wife and child of Joseph Budd, hatter
——— Bulledet
Susannah Budd, widow
Sarah Busier
Widow Bulem
Joseph Bullock's son George, and daughter Angelina
Mary Bullman
Samuel Bullman's wife
Mary Bunting
Rachel Bunting
Joseph Buffington's daughter
Joshua Bunn
Joseph Burden's child
Susannah Burden, in the Alms-house
Thomas Burden, tailor
Catharine Burkhart, a widow, Æt. 80
Margaret Burkhards
George Burdy, tailor
William Burkhard's daughter and son
Daniel Burkhard's daughter
John Burkhard and son
Elizabeth Burke
Peter Burke's daughter
George Burke's child
Catharine Burke's daughter
Joseph Burke, clerk
Margaret, wife of John Burke
Joseph Burke, from W. Indies
Thomas Burke's wife
David Burk, tailor
Sophia Burke
Jacob Burkellow, jun.
Joshua Burns, house-carpenter
Mary Burns
Patrick Burns, labourer
Elizabeth Burngate, shopkeeper
Mrs. Burns
John Burns
Thomas Burn's wife
Moses Burnet, ferryman

Robert Burrows
Elizabeth Burs
John Bufyman
William Butler, chairmaker
Elizabeth Bufh
Robert Bufby
Andrew Buttonfile's wife
Elizabeth and Clariffa Bufhell,
   daughters of John Bufhell
William Butts, fhoemaker
John Butler
Francis Byerly, a lad
John Burns, currier, and wife
Sarah Cable, a fervant
Catharine Cabler
Hannah Cadwallader
Paul Cake's wife
Sufannah Cake
James Calbraith, jun.
James Calbraith's young man
John Calder, fhopkeeper, and
   wife
John Caldwell, a child
Mary Cale
James Callagher, feaman
Martin Callaghan
Michael Calup's child and hired
   fervant
Daniel Calley
William Cameron, innkeeper
Charlotte Camp
Matthias Camp
Wife of Mr. Campbell, tailor
Ann Campbell
George Campbell, wife Sarah,
   and daughter Mary
Chriftiana Campbell
James Campbell, fhoemaker
John Campbell, fervant
Alexander Cambler
Patrick Camble, labourer
Alexander Cambell
William Campbell and wife
James Camus
Gilmet Cambay
Daniel Canaaen, blackfmith,
   and child, Ir.
John Candie
Mary Cane, widow
John Canner, baker
Phebe Cane
James Cannon
Fanny Cannon

George Capehart, tobacconift
George Capehart and child
Frederic Capehart, apprentice
Caleb Cappey
Chriftopher Carefoot
Francis Cardell
Eleanor Carrell
Catharine Care
Laurence Carrell, brafs-founder
Andrew Care, tailor
Philip Care's wife and child
Peter Carey, apprentice
John Carey's child
Peter Carey's child
—— Carey's wife
Stelena Carl
Thomas Carnes, paper-hanger
Andrew Carney, blackfmith
Bernard Carpentier
John Carpenter
James Carper
John Carner
Hannah Carlwine
James Carr, labourer, and wife
John Carr
Jofeph Carr, joiner, and wife
Jofeph Carr, apprentice
Rebecca Carr and mother
Mary Carr
Rob't Carr's wife, brafs-founder
Daniel Carrigan, bricklayer
Charles Carroll, merchant
Elizabeth Carrens
Mary Carrol
Sarah Carrowood, fervant
Timothy Carrell
William Carfs, tailor
William Carfs and child
Ann Carfon, houfe-wife
Francis Carfon, labourer
Jofeph Carfon
Jofeph Caffin
Hannah Carter
Lewis Carter, harnefs-maker
James Carter
James Carter, jun.
John Carpenter's daughter
Jacob Cathrall, fon of Ifaac
Benjamin Cathrall's fon
William Cathers
Catharine ——, a fervant
Julian Catton

David Cay, merchant
Chriftian Cent
Frederic Cephers, joiner
Mary Francis Chabot
—— Chace, of Baltimore
Dorothy Chafferly
Abraham Chalwell
David Chambers, ftone-cutter
Adam Chambers's child
Henrietta Chambers
Harriet Chamberlaine's daugh.
Richard Chamberlaine's daugh.
Sarah Chambers
Dorothy Chapman
James Chapman, whip-maker
Hannah Chapman
Charles ——, a drover
John Chatham, blackfmith
Nicholas Chatt
Claudius Chatt
Thomas Cherry, cooper
Mary Cherry
George Chefs's wife
Eliza Chefter
Thomas Chevalier
Michael Chew's child
William Chipley
Ernft Chrift
Jacob Chriftler's wife
Elizabeth Chriftie
Matthew Chriftie, fen.
Matthew Chriftie, jun.
Andrew Chriftie, printer
Polly Chriftie
Frederic Chriftian, baker
George Chrifthelf's daughter,
  and her child
Maria Chriftly
Samuel Chriftman
Johann Chriftmann's fon Johann
James A. Chubb
George Chrifthelf, mufician
John Chriftel's fon
John Clackworthy
Adam Clamper, and child
Thomas Clamper
Ann Clampton
Ferdinand Clancy
Abijah Clark's child

James Clark, carpenter
Nelly Clark
Margaret Clark
Chriftian Clark's young man
Thomas Clark, brickmaker
Edward Clark
Sarah Clark
William Clark, waterman
James Clarkfon
Margaret Clafpin
John Clatworthy, tailor
George Claufe
David Claypoole's two children
George Claypoole, joiner
William Claypoole's child
Bartley Clayton's child
Francis Clayton
Benjamin Clayton
William Claw
Elizabeth Clements
Chloe ——, fervant
William Clements
Jacob Clements, farmer
Mary Clements and fon
Samuel Clements, New-Jerfey
Thomas Cleverly, baker
Thomas Clifford, fen. merchant
Sarah Clifton
Ifaac Clime, carpenter
Sophia Climer
Daniel Cline, baker
David Cline and daughter
Ifaac Cline, carpenter
Devolt Cline
George Cline
John Cline, labourer
John Cline, bricklayer
Philip Cline, baker
Mrs. Clingham
Mary Clingland
Church Clinton, houfe carpen-
  ter, and wife
Margaret Clofter
Andrew Clow, merchant
William Clow, printer
George Clowfe
James Clubb
Philip Clumberg, furg. barber
Chriftian Cluper

Hugh Clymer
Daniel Coarigan, bricklayer
Jofiah Coates's daughter Margaret
Thomas Coates's child
Wife and child of John Cobble, blackfmith
John Coburn's child
Samuel Whiteafe Coburn
Child of James Cochran, houfe carpenter
John Cocklin
John Cochran, a feaman
Mrs. Cohen and fon George
Thomas Colbert, clerk
Jofeph Coleman's wife
William Coleman's child
Dorothy Coleman
Adam Collins, tobacconift
Honora Collins and child
Judith Collins, fervant
Nicholas Collins, trunk-maker
Margaret Collins
Ralph Collins and wife
William Collins, his wife, his two daughters, his fecond wife, his fon James, his wife, & his child, all of one family
Ifaac Collins
Catharine Collyer
Sarah Coltman, midwife
John Colvill's child
Sarah Colway
Abraham Camby, carpenter
Cornelius Comegys' wife Ann
Mary Commyns
Sarah Commyns
Robert Conckell
Barbara Conard
Margt. Conard, daugh. of John
Mary Conard
Maria Conde's fon
Matthew Conard, tavern-keeper
Robert Condit
Margaret Conery
Michael Conrad, a lad
John Conrad, and wife
Mrs. Conrad, and girl
John Conrad, watchman
Widow Conrad
Maria Conrad
Jane Conkey
George Connelly, bricklayer
George Connelly's child
John Connelly's child

Molly, daughter of Michael Conner
Sarah Connelly
Patrick Connelly
Margaret, wife of Jofeph Conyers
—— Confer, tailor
Charles Contant
Edward Cook's daughter
George Cook, labourer, & wife
Henry Cook
Henry Cook
George Cook, porter
William Cook, ftone-cutter
James Cook
John Cook
William Cook's child
George Cowper's wife
Jacob Cowper, apprentice
John Cooper's apprentice
James Cooper, labourer
Peter Cowper's fon, currier
William Cowper, currier
Charles Cope, fhoemaker
Son of John Cope, butcher
George Cope
Margaret Conry
Jacob Coppas, labourer
Patt. Conly
Michael Corroy
James Cornelius, carpenter
David Copeland, tavern-keeper
Mrs. Corns, and fon
Mrs. Corran
Mary Cone
Lewis Coffart, apprentice
William Corfy
Michael Corley, upholfterer
Nicholas Corley, mill-ftone maker, and child
Judith Corley
Lewis Coul
Elizabeth Corkrin
John Cotringer
William Roulfon, fawyer
Richard Courtney, tailor
John Coufins, ftore-keeper
Widow Cownouft's child
John Cowen, ftore-keeper
James Cowan and child
John Coward, hemp-dreffer
William Cowles
Samuel Cowty's child
Louifa Cowell
Barney Cox

John Cox, fhoemaker
William Cox
The boy and girl of William Cox, chair-maker
Jofeph Cox, currier
—— Cox's fon-in law
Alexander Cox
Charles Cox's child
Jofeph Cox, and wife
Ann Coy
John Cozens
Jacob Craft, breeches maker
James Coffee
William Coffee
Dennis Connor
Rebecca Corron
Anthony Cradet
James Craig, merchant, Æt. 80
Edward Crane
John Craig's wife
Lydia Craig
Mrs. Craig
Mrs. Craig
Jacob Cramp, bifcuit-baker
Sufannah Cramp
George Craps
James Crawford's child
Chrif. Crawlinberg, joiner
Margaret Craig, widow
Mary Crayhead, feamftrefs
Henry Creemer
Cafper Crefs, and daughter
Andreas Creffman's fervant
Margaret Crefs
Caleb Creffon's wife
Jofhua Creffon, merchant
Peter Creffon
Lewis Crefly's wife
Chriftian Chriffwell's child
Elizabeth Criffwell
Chriftopher Criel's fon
John Croll, barber
—— Cronow, fugar-boiler
Catharine Crofs
—— Cromwell's wife
Daniel Crofs, carpenter, & wife
Daniel Crofs, jun. carpenter
Fanny Crofs, wafherwoman
Peter Crofs
Mary Crofs's child
George Crow, brafs-founder
Henry Crowell's wife

John Crowley, potter
James Crowley
Mary Crowley and daughter
John Crubreux, drayman
Mr. Crull's child
Wife of John Crumb, bricklayer
Philip Cruncle
John Crump's child
Paul Cuckot
Catharine Cunan
Ann Cunningham
Robert Cunningham's child
Comfort Cunningham
Hannah Cunningham
Michael Cunningham
Matthew Cunningham
Peter Curren's' child
Mrs. Currens, and two fons
Mercy Currie
James Currie
Rebecca Currier
Ann Curtain
Thomas Cuftard, fhoemaker
Jacob Daderman's child
Robert Dainty, plumber
Bridget Daily
Capt. Richard Dales's child
Peter Dale's daughter Sarah
Francis Dalmafe
Thomas Dabriel, fhoemaker
John Dalton, clockmaker
David Damfen, fhoemaker
Julian Danacker
George Danecker, and wife
Robert Dannell
Catharine Dardis
Henry Darroch, ftore-keeper
John Daum, labourer
Conrad Dauenhaer's daughter
George Daum's wife
John David, filverfmith
Ann David
Robert Davidfon
James Davidfon, merchant
James Davidfon's child
Ifaac Daves
Capt. Davis's two nephews
Elizabeth Davis
Gilford Davis's wife
Ifaac Davis's wife
John Davis, wheelwright, wife and daughter

S

Joseph Davis, labourer
Joseph Davis, soap-boiler
Mary Davis's child
Michael Davis
Robert Davis, anchor-smith
Samuel Davis
Hester, wife of Sam. Davis, sen.
Sophia Davis
Susannah Davis
Rachel, wife of Joseph Davis, currier
Widow Davis
Widow Davis
William Davis
John Davis, upholsterer
Richard Davy
Mary Dawkens
Hannah Dawson
Joshua Dawson's child
Daniel Dawson's wife Hannah
Mary Dawson
Darius Dawson
James Day's wife
Elizabeth Day
Sarah Days
Edward Deal, blacksmith
John Deal, blacksmith
Mary Deal, servant
Peter Deal's child
Margaret Dean
Joseph Dean, vendue-master, a woman and child
Patrick Deary
Joseph de Barth
Mr. Deberger, his wife, and 6 or 7 of the family
Jacob Debre
Elizabeth Debre
Thomas Debzel
Christian Deckard
John C. Deckard, musician
Christ. Deckenhart, apprentice
Henry Decker, a servant
Jenny Degenhart
Christopher Degenhard & child
Wilhelmina Degenhard
William Deganhort
Ann D. Deiss
Benjamin Delany, chair-maker
Henry Delany
Dennis Delany's child

John Delany
Patrick Delany's child
Bridget Delay, cook
Samuel Delap, bookseller
John Demaffrand's daughter
Andrew Denahaw, cooper
Mary Denckla, a child
Richard Denney
Mary Denny
Robert Dennet, groom
Ezekiah Denum
William Dennis
George Dennison
George Densell
Henry Densell's wife
Maria Denzell
Henry Depherwinn's son
George Dernberger
Henry Derham
James Derry
Widow Deringer
Adam Detterick, shoemaker
John Devenny's child
Christian Devir
Thomas Devonald, merchant
Margaret Dewis
Campbell Dick, merchant
John Dibberger, cutler, and wife
Charlotte Dibberger
Henry Dibberger, sen. and wife
John Dickz's son
Dick ——, a negro, aged 75
John Dickenson, bookbinder
Mary Dickinson
Jonathan Dickinson, shoemaker
—— Dickinson, drover
Daniel Dickenson's daughter
Elizabeth Dickinson
William Dickinson
John Dickinson's child
P. Dickinson's daughter Maria
Thomas Dickinson's wife
William Dickinson, farmer
Michael Dignon and two sons
Edward Diehl, smith
John Diehl's son, porter
Maria M. Diehl
John Diehl, carpenter
Henry Dietz, baker
John Dietmar, labourer
Maria Dietz

Elizabeth Dietrick
Michael Dietrick's son
William Dieu, a child
Frederick Dillman's wife
Catharine Dill's child
Mr. Dingle's child
Jane Dight, a servant
Catharine Dorothy Dirrick
William Dallas
Christian Dishong, and child
Maurice Dishong, clerk
Matthew Dishong's child
Susannah Dishong, widow
John Dixon's wife
Elizabeth Dixon
Patrick Dixon's child, labourer
William Dixon, joiner
Doctor John Dodd
Jacob Doddelmah's wife and
   two children
Dolly, a black woman
Julian Doison
John Doll, carpenter
Hugh Donaldson, son of John
Arthur Donaldson's son
John Donahue
Johanna Donahue
Abigail Donahue
Margaret Donnelly
Philip H. Dorneck
William Dorr
Sarah H. Dorsey
Robert Dorsey's servant girl
William Doudney
Barnard Dougherty
Jeremiah Dougherty, carpenter
John Dougherty, carpenter
Rev. William Dougherty
Margaret Dougherty, servant
Henry Dougherty
Elizabeth Doughty
Charlotte Douglass
G. W. Douglass, silver-smith
Joseph Douglass, hair-dresser
William Douglass, carter
Peggy Dougney
Mary Dove
Thomas Dowling
Nathaniel Dowdry, carpenter
Mrs. Down
William Downey, whip-maker
Nathaniel Downing

Peter Doyle
James Doyle
Mary Doyle
Henry Drawiller
John Drieux, wife & daughter
William Drinker
Elizabeth Driscall and child
John B. Drouillard's 2 children
John Drum's child
Eleanor Drum
Cha. Fk. Dubois, watch-maker
Joseph Dubreez's wife
Erenna Duffield
Lucy Duffield
J. Dufour's daughter Catharine
Nancy Dugan and child
William Duglas
Du Lac, French ambassador's
   secretary
———— Dull, hatter
Charles Dunbar
John Dunbury, servant
John Dudman
James Duncan's wife and child
John Dunkin, merchant
John Dunleavy
Cormick Dunleavy
Margaret Dunley, servant
Ann Dunn
Elizabeth Dunn
Sarah Dunn
Francis Dupail
Doctor Joseph Dupac
Elizabeth Duplessis
Francis Dupont, consul of
   French republic
Philip Durnick
John Durker
Peter Durieu
Rosanna Durang
Joseph Duvet
John Durney's child
Thomas Durnell's daughter
Susannah Dyes
William Earl
Grace Easlaugh and child
Charles Eastick
Sarah Eastick
John Eastick's wife
George Eborne's child
John P. Eck, grocer
Elizabeth Eccles

James Eccles's two daughters
———Eccles
George Eckel, linen-draper
Mary Eccles
Elizabeth Eccles
Deborah Eckley
John Ecky's apprentice
——— Eckstein's wife Catharine
and child
Maria Echard
Philip Edenborn, carpenter
Phil. Edenborn, flour-merchant
John Edmundson
Edward Edwards's two children
Ephraim Edwards, labourer
John Edwards, sailor
Abigail Edwards's child
Morgan Edwards, hatter
John Edwards
Samuel Edwards and wife
William Edwards, silversmith,
and child
Catharine Egan
James Eggar
Martin Ehrhard's daughter
Elizabeth Ehrenzellers
Jacob Ehringer
Mary Eidenfield, servant
Ann Eiler
John Eisenbrey, tavern-keeper
Richard Elber's child
Francis Elcock
David Elder, clerk
Sarah Elder
David Elder and wife
John Element, coachman
J. Elfrey, cooper, wife & child
Catharine Elfry
Josiah Elfrith, joiner
Laurence Ellers and wife
William Ellery
Isaac Elliot
John Elliot
Mary Elliot
Hannah Ellis
Elizabeth Ellis and child
Samuel A. Ellis
Ann Elmore
Margt. Elmslie, from Scotland
Sarah Ellsworth

Joseph Elum, merchant
Elsy, a black
Andrew Elwine
Hannah Elwins, a child
Baitzer Emerick's two sons
Lætitia Emuel
Maria Emelott
Widow Emmeret
Jacob Enk, tailor, & 3 sons, viz
Philip Enk, teller in B. U. S.
Henry Enk, linen-draper
Peter Enk, tailor
Jacob Endre's brother in-law
Catharine Enger, and child
Christian Englehot, labourer
James Engles's child
John Engles, merchant
John English
Jacob Erringer, weaver
Peter Erston, wife & 2 chidre
Anthony John Escorcio, clerk
Frederic Esker, baker
Christian Esling
Barbara Esky
Jacob Essler, blacksmith
Margaret Estling
George Eswin's wife
Adam Etner
Elizabeth Ettrick
Matthew Ettrick's wife
Ettienne J. Eude's child
John Evans's child
Magdalen Evans
Joseph Evans
Mary Evans
James Evans
Mary Evans, a hired girl
Nancy Evans
Philip Evans, house-carpenter
Phillis Evans
Rowland Evans, merchant
Rowland Evans
Israel Everly, shoemaker
Widow Eberman
Anthony Everhardt, labourer
William Evil
John Ewen's two children
Thomas Ewing's two childre
John Eysenbry, tavern-keepe
Henry Facundus, shoemaker
and wife

John Fairus, ship-carpenter
Mary Faires
Arthur Falconer, Jr.
Hannah Falkenburger, Germ.
Casper Farner's wife
Joseph Farren, jun.
John Farren
Edward Farren's child
John Farrow, shoemaker
John Fasler
Michael Fatty's two children
John Fauser's son
William Favel, baker
Samuel Faringer's wife
Charles Fearis, seaman
Tobias Febias
Widow Feller's child
Jacob Felty, Germ.
Felix Fenner, labourer
Daniel Fenance, a child
Joseph Fenny
Daniel Fenton, shoemaker, and wife
David Fenton, shoemaker, and wife
Thomas Fenton, jun.
Philip T. Fentham, druggist
Widow Fenton
Thomas Fenton, sail-maker
Ferely, widow
Widow Ferglass
Elizabeth Ferguson
Samuel Ferguson
Robert Ferguson, brick-layer
Thomas Ferguson, printer
Barnabas Ferris, clerk
John Ferris
Francis Ferris, clerk
Ann Margaret Fidlers, widow
Barbara Field
Charles Field, chair-maker
Peter Field's wife
Widow Filler
Thomas Fielder
Catharine Fiete
William Fimister, farmer
Francis Finley
Charles Findley, grave-digger
Jane Findley
Michael Finn's child

William Finn, hatter
Charles Finney's daughter
Joseph Finney
John Fink, porter
Charles Fink, shoemaker
Hannah Firmir
William Firm
William Finister
Ann Fisher, servant
Catharine Fisher, servant
David Fisher, labourer
Jabez, son of Miers Fisher
John Fisher
Robert Fisher
Henry Fisher, starch-maker, and wife
Patrick Fisher, shoemaker
John Fisher and daughter
Samuel Fisher, button-plater, Eng.
Zachariah Fisher's child
Samuel Fisher, hatter
Sarah Fisher, servant
Samuel Fishinger's wife
Jacob Fisler, tailor
Anthony Fisler
Jacob Fisler, labourer, and wife
Christopher Fite, shoemaker, Germ.
Adam Fister, carpenter
Margaret Fitzgerald
William Fitzgerald, tailor
Gerald Fitzsimmons
Jeremiah Fitzsimmons, painter
John Fitzsimmons
Philip Flack, joiner
George Flauer's daughter
George Fleck's wife
Jacob Fleck's six children
Reverend Francis A. Fleming, catholic clergyman
Margaret Fleini
Hugh Fleming, tavernkeeper
Hugh Fleming, son of do.
Samuel Fleming, sen.
Samuel Fleming, jun.
Elizabeth Fletcher
Charles Flick, wife and child
David Flickwir, confectioner, wife, and son

James Flinn
Mary Flinn
Anne Flint, widow
Flora, a black girl
Monf. Florio, Fr.
Margaret Flour
George Flowers's child
Eliza. Faggle
Mary Faggle, daughter of do.
William Faggle
Elizabeth Follows, widow
Widow Folwell's child
Ifaac I. Folwell, tailor
Daniel Ford, farmer
George Forde's child
George Ford, hoftler
Fortune Ford
Alexander Foreman's daughter
John Forefter
William Forefter, labourer
John Forfe
Thomas Forfter, hatter
Nicholas Fofberg, church-clerk
Nicholas Fofberg, fen. painter
Ann Fofter
Margaret Foffom, Germ.
Wife of George Founce, fisher-
    man
Lemuel Fowles and child
George Fowme, fisherman
William Fowles, mufician
Dorothy Fox
Robert Fox
George Fox and three children
George Fox
Garret Foyer
Frederic Foy
James Frampton
George France
Jofeph France
Rebecca Francis
Jacob Franks's wife
David Franks
David S. Franks, affiftant ca-
    fhier of the U. S. B.
Catharine Fraim
Elizabeth Frafer, in the Widows'
    Hofpital
Mary Frafer
Robert Frafer
John Frederick, labourer
Anthony Freeborn, shoemaker

Jacob Freeborn, tobacconift.
Tobias Freeborough
Tobias Freebush, shoemaker
Ifaac Freeman
Jacob Freneau
Catharine Freeth, fervant
Philip Fries, labourer
William French
Sufannah French, nurfe
Charles French's daugh. Eliza.
7 French ftrangers (names un-
    known)
Michael Frick, carter
Jacob Frilander, labourer
Abry Friend, negro
Elizabeth Friend
John Fritz, tailor
John Fritz, tavern-keeper
Elizabeth Froft
Jofeph Fromp, apprentice
James Fruger
Jacob Fry, apprentice
Jane Fry
Mary Fry, wife of Jofeph Fry
Jofeph Fry, junior
George Fudge's wife, & daugh.
John Fagle, wife, and two fons
Jacob Fulton
Widow Fuller
Henry Furgurfon, tailor, and
    wife
William Fuffelback's child
Peter Gabriel, baker
Ferdinand Gabriel
Mary Gabriel
Sarah Gainer
Mary, daugh. of Ja's Gallagher
Daniel Gallagher
Ally Gallagher
Michael Gallimore, farmer
Sarah Galloway, Æt. 75
Mary Ann Gally
Elizabeth Galler
Catharine Gallinger
John Gamber's child
John Gambles's wife
Mary Ganno
Elizabeth Gans
Drufilla Gardner
Michael Garcoin
Elizabeth Gardner

Elizabeth Gardner, fervant
Wife of James Gardner, failor
John Gardner, fhoemaker
Mary Gardner
Richard Gardner, tea-dealer
Benjamin Gardener
Widow Margaret Gardner
Mr. —— Garre
Andrew Garter
John Gartner, labourer
Mary Garret
Thomas Garrette, apprentice
Elizabeth Garret
Thomas Garrigues, hatter
Samuel Garrigues's wife & fon
Andrew Gartley
John Gartly
Sarah Gaffner
Valentine Gafner's daughter
Gafper Gafner, fhoemaker, fon
  and daughter
George Gafner's fon
John Gartly
Andrew Gatley
William Gauflin
Adolph Gaul, butcher
Jofeph Gaven
John Gawn, tailor and child
Widow Gebhard and daughter
Rachel Gebhard
Dorothy Geir
Chriftian Genfel, porter
John Gelher, labourer
Wife of John Genther, tailor
George Genflin's child
Margaret Genther
Robert George
Michael Gering's child
John Getts, plafterer, and wife
Jacob Geyer, tailor
Ifaac Geyer's fon
Henry Gibert, cabinet-maker
John Gibard
Margaret Gibfon, and child
Andrew Gibfon's wife
Mary Ann Gibfon
Robert Gibfon, cabinet-maker
Nancy Gibfon
George Gilberts wife
Michael Gilbert, potter
Ruth Gilbert

Sarah Gilbert, fervant
James Gilchrift, merchant, Eng.
William Gilfrey's wife
John Gill, tallow-chandler, &
  child
Jofeph Gill
Sarah Gill
John Gillingham
Mary Gillingham, fpinfter
Mrs. Girard
Mrs. Gilmore
Margaret Ginther
John Ginther, tailor, and wife
William Girtin
Mr. Gifm
Ferdinand Glancey, labourer
Nathaniel Glover, merchant
Elizabeth Glynn
Benjamin Glynn
Peter Glentworth, phyfician
Michael Gleenfon's child
John Gobblegought, Germ.
Mary Godin
William Godfrey
—— Golden, hair-dreffer, Boft.
Martha Goldfmith, widow
Thomas Goldrick
Henry Goldfon, apprentice
Henry Golzer
John Good, labourer, Germ.
Jofeph Good, wife and child
Mary Good, from Bucks county
Michael Good, brickmaker
Mofes Goodman, labourer
George Goodman's child
James Goodwin
Abraham Gordon, carpenter
Elizabeth Gordon
John Gordon, Ir.
Peter Gordon, fhoemaker
Enoch Gordon
Richard Goren's child
Michael Gorran
James Gorham, carpenter and
  button-maker
William Gofling, houfe-carpen-
  ter
Catharine Gofner, Germ.
Jofeph Gofner, jun.
Sarah Gofner, fervant
John Gotze, plafterer, and wife

Morris Gough, ship-carpenter, wife and two children
James Gowan, sailor
Joseph Gowan
George Grace, labourer
Jacob Grace's wife
Rev. Laurence Graefsl, catholic pastor
Batty Graff's child
John Graff's wife
Jacob Graff, mason
Thomas Graham
Dr. Graham, late of New York
Robert Graham
Duncan Graham, carpenter
Mary Graham
John Graham, stone-cutter
Casper Graist's daughter
Jonathan Grammer
William Grant, tailor
Alexander Graves's wife
Ludwick Graver's child
William Gravenstone
John Gray, rope-maker
Peter Gray's child
Joseph Gray
Thomas Gray, jun.
Robert Greaves, hair-dresser
George Greble, cooper
Elizabeth Green and child
Edward Green, ship-carpenter
Michael Green
James Green's wife & daughter
Susanna Greens
John Green's child
John Green, labourer, Ir.
Isaac Green, labourer
John Green
Solomon Green, tobacconist
William Grenville
Levander Greff
John Greenward
Benjamin Greiner, nailor
Archibald Greenlap
John Greisberger's wife
Ann Gergory, widow, Æt. 60
Malcolm Gregory
Thomas Gregory, cooper
Christian Gregory's child
Ann Gregg
John Grehaut, labourer
John Gribble

George Gribble, cooper
Jonathan Grice, shipwright
Joseph Grieve's wife
John Grier, and wife
Thomas Grissiner
Mary Griez, widow, Æt. 63
Levander Griffee
Mary Griffen
Sellwood Griffin, blockmaker
William Griffin
Margaret Grindle
John Griffin
Samuel Griscam, carpenter
Rebecca Griscam, wife of do.
Casper Grisgam, sawyer, Ir.
Ann Griggs
William Griggen
Sam. Griskel, carpenter, & wife
Catharine Grogan
John Gross's wife
Widow Gross
Widow Grossings
Joseph Groves, tailor
Jacob Groves, blacksmith
Margaret Groves
John Grubb, carpenter
John Grubb, jun. carpenter
James Grumman's child
John Gryce, sail-maker
Henry Guel
Geo. Gucneau's wife, & child
Mr. —— Guerre
John Guest, sen.
Judas Guier
Marcus Gunn
Neil Gunn, labourer
Daniel Gurney's child
William Guiton, and wife
James Guthrie, carpenter
John Gutts, plasterer, and wife
Jacob Gueyer, son of ditto
Frederic Haas
Matthew Hass
Mary Hass
John Habear
Catharine Hasline, spinster
Daniel Hasline, blacksmith
William Haft, shoemaker, wife, and apprentice
Susanna Haga
Catharine Hagar
S. Hagelgans, stocking-weaver

Valentine Hagner, fen. cooper
Valentine Hagner, junior
Elizabeth Hagner
Andreas Haidt, fmith
Andreas Haft
Wm. Haft, fhoemaker, & wife
Samuel Hailagus, ftocking-
  weaver
David Hailer, furgeon
Frederick Hailer's wife
Widow Hailey
John Haltzel, tailor
John Haines's wife
Dorothy Hains
Reuben Haines, fen. brewer,
Margaret Haines, wife of ditto
George Hake, cooper
Jacob Halberftott
Charles Halden, hatter
Sebaftian Hale, or Ale, grave-
  digger
Thomas Hale, bell-hanger
Patrick Haley, labourer
Penelope Haley
Philip Hall, butcher, Germ.
Dorothy Hall
Parry Hall and daughter
Elizabeth Hall
John Hall
Samuel Hall, labourer, Eng.
Mrs. Haller
Philip Haller, cooper
John Hallet, hair-dreffer, and
  wife
Charles Hallick's fifter
Anthony Haman
Charles Hambleton's wife
Henry Hambleton
Abraham Hambright's wife
Jofeph D. Hamelin, French
  tutor
Alexander Hamilton's wife
James Hamilton
John Hamilton, apprentice
Mary Hamilton
William Hamilton
Unity Hammel
Margaret Hammon
Jacob Hammond, fugar-baker,
  wife and child, Germ.
Nicholas Hampftead's fon and
  daughter

Elizabeth Hampftead
Child of Samuel Hampton, gro-
  cer
Thomas Hampton
Michael Hanaghan, fervant
John Hanks's maid
Capt. Jacob Hand's widow
George Haney, carpenter, and
  wife
John Haney, labourer, Ir.
John Hannah and child
Jofeph Hanna, tailor
Chriftian Hanna
Andrew Hanna
William Hannan
Wife of Barnet Hanfell, tailor
Andrew Hanifh
Mr. Hanfell, Germ.
Wife of Chriftian Hanfeman,
  tailor
John Haragel, baker
Thomas Harden
Eve Harding
James Harding, fawyer
Hannah Harding
William Hardinefs's wife
James Hardy
Jane Hardey
John Hare, labourer
William Harklife
Jacob Harlman and wife
Jofeph Harman, hair-dreffer
Mary-Herman
Temperance Harmer
Sarah Harmer
Alexander Harme
Nicholas Harmftadt, and daugh-
  ter
Jane Harned
Hannah Harnfey
Chriftopher Harper's daughter
Henry Harper, hair-dreffer
Mary Harper
Jofeph Harper's three children
William Harper's wife and
  child
John Harragan, tailor
Michael Harragan, fmith
Thomas Harrell, farmer
Edward Harris's wife
John Harris and wife

T

William Harris
Peale Harris
Thomas Harris, fadler
William P. Harris, clerk
Widow Harris
Elizabeth Harris
Hazel Harriot
Mary Harrifon, nurfe
Jane Harrifon
Sarah Harrifon
Margaret Harrifon
Jacob Hart, pilot
Laurence Hart, ftorekeeper
Rachel Hart
Thomas Hart, fhoemaker, Eng.
John Hartford, coachman
Sarah Hartley, Eng.
Sufanna Hartley
Anthony Hartman
Jacob Hartman, apprentice
Peter Hartman's wife
Lewis Hartman
John Hartrau's wife
Elizabeth Harvey
Elizabeth Harvey, fchoolmif-
    trefs, Eng.
Samuel Harvey, apprentice
Philip Hafenbach, labourer
Wm. Haffel, fen. tavern-keeper
Ifaac Hartings, ftudent
Lydia Hatfield
James Hattriotz, baker
Jacob Haufhaw's young woman
John Haufkins, fhoemaker
William Hautzel, weaver
——— Haufman's daughter
Henry Hauften
Chriftian Hautzel, carter
Chriftopher Haufer's wife
Jacob Hawes.
Anna Maria Hawan
Hugh Hawthorn, tailor
Mary Hawthorn
William Hays, ironmonger
Michael Hay, wife, and three
    fons, John, Peter, and Charles
Jofeph Hay
Martha Hays,
Jacob Hays
Mary Hays, of Allentown
Catharine Hayes, a ftranger

John Haynes, apprentice
Catharine Haynes
Ruth Haynes
Hannah Hazard
James Hazelet, weaver, Ir.
Charles Hazzleton
John Heartenough's wife
Chrif. Heatley, merchant's wife
Harriot, wife of Charles Heatly
George Heck, cooper
Samuel Head's daughr. Mary
——— Hebert, a Frenchman
Anthony Hecht, labourer
Charles Heitberger, butcher
John Helm's child
Jacob Heiberger's child
George Heiberger's fon
John Heiberger, baker
Roger Heffernan
John Heffernan, fchool-mafter
William Heifzer, painter
Widow Heil
John Heil's child
Anna Maria Heintzen
John Heifer, hatter
Francis Helfrick's wife & child
Elizabeth Held
Peter Helt's wife
Catharine Hem
James Hendrick, fen. cutler
James Henderfon's wife
Redmond Henderfon
Thomas Henderfon's child
Mary Henderfon
Ann Hendrick
Wilhelmina Hedrick, and fou
    fervants
Elizabeth Hedrick
Martha Hemphill
John Henna
Patrick Hennabody, coach-ma-
    ker, wife and daughter
John Henan's child
Michael Hennafey
John Henigel, baker
John Henry, jeweller
Margaret Henry
Chriftopher Henfner's daugh.
Wife of Henry Henfon, brufh-
    maker
Michael Henfzey
George Hercules, a negro

William Hercules, shoemaker
Elizabeth Herleman --
George Herman, baker
George Herlemin
William Herman's wife
William Hertzog, labourer
Christopher Herrely, labourer
John Herrill
Wife of Nicholas Hess, black-smith
George Hess's sister
Isaac Heston
—— Hetnick, baker
Israel Hewlings, shoemaker
Joseph Hewlings, bricklayer
Henry Hewmes, coppersmith
John Huson, sailor
Mrs. Hewit
Andrew Hews
John Heyberger, jun.
Mary Heyberger
John Heyburn
Andrew Heyd's son
Benja. Hickman's wife & son
David Hickman, clerk
Joseph Hicks, gluemaker
John Hicks
Richard Hicks
John Hierson, hatter
William Hickert's wife
John Jacob Hiertman, malster
Angel Higgenbottom
William Higgenbottom
Joseph Higgins
Mary Hightson
Susannah Higgin, widow
Martin Hilderburn, sieve-maker
Wife of George Hill, clerk
Robert Hill
Wife of Jacob Hill, fisherman
James Hill, bricklayer
James Hill, clerk
John Hill, chair-maker
Johannah Hill, jun.
John Hill's daughter
Samuel Hill, Ir.
James Hillman, apprentice
Jacob Hillman, blacksmith
Catharine Hillner
Jacob Hilsinger, labourer
William Hiltzheimer
Mary Hinan

George Hinckel, watchman
John Hinckel's son
Christop'r Hineman's daughter
Jane Hiltridge
George Hinton, cutler
Mrs. Hirst
Mary Hirrine
George Hishatters
Samuel Hampton's son
Henry Haare, cardmaker
John Hobson, sievemaker
Barbara Hackensoffe
John Hockley, ironmonger
Elizabeth Hobson
Jeffrey Hadnet, sadler, and son
Christopher Hocknoble
Catharine Hoff
Catharine Hoffman
Regina Hoffman
Isaac Hoffman, sailor
Henry Hoffman, baker
Susanna Hoffman
Jacob Hoffner, schoolmaster, Germ.
Philip Hofner, carter
Michael Hoft's son
Edward Hogan's two children
Dr. Hodge's child
Andrew Hodge's child
Joseph Hogg, carpenter, of New-Jersey
Anna Catharina Hefflein
Jacob Holberstadt, labourer
Charles Hold, hatter
Benjamin Holden, mason
Charles Holden
Wm. Holderness's son Thomas
Samuel Holgate
William Holklow
Barbara Hollard, widow
Philip Hollard, cooper
John Holmes, farmer
Sarah Holmes, widow
Sarah
Thomas Holmes's wife
Moses Homberg, innkeeper
George Honigs
William Honck, wife and child, turner
Christopher Honey
John Honecker and wife

George Honiker's wife and child

Joseph Holton

Martha Holton

Sarah Honor, widow

George Hoochey

Sarah Hoop

John Hoover's wife

Andrew Hope, jun.

William Hope, tinman

John Hopkins, jun. silver-smith

John Hopkins's wife

Joseph Hopkins, hatter, of Virginia

Mary Hopkins

Mary Hopkins, a servant

Richard Hopkins

Thomas Hopkins, ship-joiner

Joseph Hopper, joiner

Ludwick Hopler

Christian Hopsal, labourer

Henry Hore

Henry Horne, schoolmaster, and three children

Mary Horne, Germ.

Eliz. Hornor, daughter of Benjamin

Mary Horndriver

Philip Herslepaugh, shoemaker, Winchester

William Hotts

Azariah Horton

Caleb Hoskins, of Burlington

Benjamin Houlton

Anthony Hotman

John Homtan

Winnefred Houghey's child

Catharine House, Germ.

Elizabeth Houchen

Abby Houseman

Jacob Houseman, carpenter

Joseph Houts, hair-dresser

William Houtson, weaver

John Hover's wife

Mr. Howard

John Howard, paper-maker, Eng.

Thomas Howe, rope-maker

Jacob R. Howell, notary public

Jacob S. Howell

Isaac Howell's wife Patience

Mr. Howell

Catharine Howsty

Adam Hubley, vendue-master

John Huber's child

William Hudson, wool-comber

Peter Hudson

Joseph Hudell's wife Sarah

Benjamin Huggins

Ellis Hughes, whitesmith

Caleb Hughes's child and two apprentices

Garret Hughes and wife

John, son of Hugh Henry

Henry Hughes

George Hughes's child

William Hughes, breechesmaker, Scotland

Frederic Huler, sailor's wife

Diana Hulford

Abraham Hulings' wife

Oliver C. Hull, apothecary

Joshua Humphreys, Æt. 86

Hannah Humphreys, daughter of do.

John Humphreys's child

Richard Humphreys, storekeeper

Gabriel Humphreys's child

James Hunt, clerk

William Hunt, tailor

Ann Hunter's child

John Hunter, carpenter

William Hunter, tavern-keeper and child

John Hunter's daughter

John Husey

Charles Hunsman

Mr. Hustick's child

Elizabeth Huston, seamstress

John Huston, print cutter, England

James Hutchinson, physician, his child and apprentice

George Hutamn, hair-dresser

Rebecca Hutman, a child

John Hurey

Mary Hynin

William Hyser, painter, Germ.

Maria Hyson, Germ.

Peter Ilett

John Insell's daughter Mary

————— Inglis, storeeper

John Ingles, merchant, of Yorkshire

Judith, a black woman
Juliana, a mulatto
Corneha Julio
Catharine Jung
Jacob Jung's daughter
David Juftice, apprentice
John Juftice's child
William M. Juftice, printer
Jofeph Kaenerle
Jacob Kales, labourer
John Kalkbrener's wife
Godfrey Kartis, fhoemaker
Jacob Kates, labourer
Elizabeth Katten, Carlifle
Catharine Kattz
Elizabeth Kattz and two chil-
  dren
John Kattz's wife
Ifaac Kattz's wife
Michael Kattz's child
Mary Karn
Jacob Hauffman's fon
John Kean's two children
Jofeph Kean's child
Hugh Kean's child
Mary Kean
Matthew Kean's daughter
Elizabeth Keen and child
John Keen's child
Jofeph Keen
Mary Keen
Sufannah Keigen
Elizabeth Kell
James Kellenan
George Kelly, harnefs-maker
Mrs. Kelly
Chriftopher Kellman and wife
Jofeph Kemel's fon
Henry Kemp
William Kemp
Martha Kemphill, fervant
—— Kenny
Mrs. Keppele
John Keppler, fhoemaker
William Kennedy, labourer
John Kennon
Cafper, Peter and Catharine
  Kenfinger
Thomas Kenrick, ftore-keeper
Elizabeth Kenron
John Kerbeck
William Kerls, porter

Adam Kerr's widow
Andrew Kerr, labourer
James Kerr's widow
Prude Kerr
Abigail Kefler
Jacob Kefler's wife
John Kefsler, hair-drefſer
Leonard Kefsler
Michael Kefsler, fhip-joiner
Lucy Keating
Chriſtian Keyfer, blackfmith
Daniel Keyfer, labourer
Jofeph Keyfer, grocer
Jacob Kitchlien, butcher
George Kichn's daughter
Chriſtian Kiegler
Thomas Kildrick
John Killgour
George Killinger
Peter Killinger
Philip Killinger, carpenter
Richard Killpatrick
Caleb Kimber, fchoolmafter
Aaron Kimber, fon of do.
Jacob Kimely
Wife of Cafper Kinck, fhoema
  ker
Catharine King
Charles King
Elizabeth King, widow
—— King
George King, coach-painter
Hugh King's two children
John King and child
Mary King
Jofeph Kingfleey
Margaret Kingfl
Ann Kinley
Jofeph Kinnear's child
Chriftopher Kinnefs, tailor
Chriftopher Kinns, labourer
George Kinfinger and wife
Hanah Kinfinger
—— Kipfey, furrier
Mrs. Kirk and child
John Kirk, a lad
Thomas Kirk, baker
Catharine Kite
Elizabeth Kite
Jonathan Kite, chair-mak
  wife and three children

Casper Kitts

Jacob Kitts, chandler, son and cousin

Mrs. Kitts

Catharine Klady

Margaret Klady

Widow Klepper

Christian Klibsie, weaver and child

Andrew Kline's wife

John Kline, labourer

Nicholas Klingeler, cooper

Mary Klingle

Charles Knight, biscuit-baker

Hannah Knight

John Knight, tailor

John Knight, sailor

Sarah Knight

Daniel Knodle

Elizabeth Knows, servant

Mary Knows

Adam Knox

Richard Knox's child

Mary Koan

George Kock, labourer, his wife Catharine and son

John Kock

Widow Kock

Joseph Kock

Widow Koenner

George Kor's child

Peter Krafter and daughter

Christop'r Kreyder, tobacconist

Wife of George Kribbs, shoemaker

Susannah Kribner, Æt. 70

John Kriefle, cooper

John Kroll, hair-dresser

Joachim Krenaver, labourer

Henry Krotto's child

Catharine Iotten

Barbara Krunkoster

Abraham Krup, carpenter

John Kruteer

James Kubber

Christop'r Kucher, sugar-baker

Philip Kucher, his son

Bernard Kuffler

Wife of Frederick Kuhl

George Kuhn's wife

Jacob Kuhn's wife

John Kuhn's son

Ludwig Kuhn, clerk

Widow Kuhn

Jacob Kuncle's son

Martin Kernotler

George Kurtz

Daniel Kuren, labourer

John Lack's daughter

Lætitia ———

Daniel Lafferty and child, Ir.

Matthew Lafferty's child

John Lambsback, labourer

——— Lammoron's child

Arch. Lamont's wife, and children

Mrs. Lamont, child, and journeyman

Elizabeth Lancaster

Wife and child of Joseph Lancaster, labourer, Eng.

Joseph Landre, labourer

Margaret Landress

Nancy Lane

Mrs. Lane

Margaret Lang

Edward Langman

Huson Langstroth, paper-maker

Jacob Lanteshlag

Andrew Lapp and wife

Laurence Lapp, baker

Michael Lapp, baker, and wife

James Lapsley, steward to the British ambassador

——— Lapsley's wife & daughter

——— Lapsley, shoemaker

James Lapsley, schoolmaster, and daughter Elizabeth

Patrick Larken, clerk

Ralph Larremore's wife

Mary Lasher

Patrick Lasky

Frederic Lunderbruns, surgeon-barber

Jacob Louterman's wife and two sons

George Lautinshlager's sister

Jacob Laudersliver, shoemaker

Margaret Laudersliver

Frederic Lauman

Aaron S. Laurence, clerk, and wife

Alexander Lawrence, sen. merchant

Alexander Lawrence, jun. merchant

Archibald Lawrence's child
Charles Lawrence
Cherry Lawrence's wife
Chriſtopher Lawrence
Jacob Lawrence's two children
John Lawrence's wife
Joſeph Laurence, apprentice
Rachel Lawrence
Sarah Lawrence
Thomas Lea, merchant
J. T. Lea, ſon of do.
Thomas Leach, cabinet-maker
Margaret Leake, mantua-maker
Widow Lear's child
John Lebering's wife
Paul Leck, labourer
Francis J. Lector
Ann Lee
George Lee, apprentice
Joſeph Lee, wife, and ſon Geo.
Mary Lee
Thomas, ſon of Duncan Leech
George Lees, tailor, wife, three
   children, and two other per-
   ſons (names unknown)
John Lees, tailor
Margaret Lees
Joſeph Le Feore
William Lehman's wife
Doctor John Leibert, junior
Mic. Leibrand, breeches-maker
Mathias Leigh, labourer
Michael Leigh
Robert Leigh
John Leighy's child
Andrew Leinaw, ſadler
Samuel Leller
James Lenox, apprentice
Abner Leonard
Sarah Leonard
Francis Leſher, coach-maker
Francis Leſher, tavern-keeper
   and ſervant girl
Philip Leſher's wife
———— Letzinger's wife
George Letzinger's wife
Andrew Letton, ſhoemaker
John Letton
Moſes Levy's girl
Thomas Levy's wife
———— Lewis's child
Catharine Lewis

Jonathan, ſon of Mordecai Lew-
   is, merchant
Iſaac Lewis, tailor and wife
Lydia Lewis, widow
Maria Lewis, mulatto
Mary Lewis
Michael Lewis's ſon
William Lewis, hairdreſſer
George Lex, butcher
Jacob Lex's child
Widow Leybrandt
Chriſtian Lickett
Robert Lidler
Peter Ligert
Samuel Lilly, ſailor
John Limeburner's child
Mary Lindall
Ruth Lindill
Thomas Lindall, carter
Elizabeth Lindſay
Heſter Lindſay
Mary Lindſay
Suſannah Lindſay
Philip Linion, bottler
George Linkinſon, labourer
Elizabeth Linkfelt
Margaret Linn, Scotland
Neal Linn
William Linnar, porter
Wm. Linton, wife and ſiſter
Widow Lintz
Hannah Liſburn, widow
Miſs ——— Liſler
James Leſper
Joſeph Liſpar
Catharine Liſt
William Lethworth's child
John Littman, ſon, & daughter
Catharine Lloyd
Daniel Lloyd, apprentice
William Lloyd
Wood Lloyd, tilor
Mary Lobdell
Samuel Lobdell, carpenter
John Lob's child
Elizabeth Locke, widow
———— Loeffler's wife
John Loh, and daughter
William Lohman, rope-maker
Wife of Peter Lobra, broker
Ralph Loimer, ſailor
Patrick Lollar's boy

Herman Jos. Lombaert, mer.
Frederic Long
John Long, labourer, & son
Richard Long, apprentice
William Long, joiner
Joseph Lopez, servant to the Spanish ambassador
Hannah Lorton, servant
Abraham Lott, merchant
—— Louis, Fr.
Elizabeth Lovett
George Lovett's son
John Lowden, ferryman
Rebecca Lowden
Thomas Lowden's wife
James Lowne
Edward Lowder
Sarah Lowder
William Lowman
Agnes Lownes
Ed. Lowry, labourer, & wife
Hester Lucas
Christopher Luckarts, carter, and wife
John Martin Ludwig, butcher
Thomas Ludwig
Robert Lumsden, corder
George Luntz's daughter
Lewis H. Luring, wife, & child
Widow Luring
Jacob Lusely, labourer
Elizabeth Lushinger
William Lushworm, labourer
Catharine Lutz, Germ.
Christian Lutz's child
Ann Lyland
Benjamin Lyndall's child
John Lynn, physician, of New England
Mary Lynn
Mrs. —— Lynn
Mary Lyons
Michael Lyons, sailor
Philip Maad, labourer
Jacob Macker's child
Peter Mack's wife
John Maidscaw
Daniel M'Allister
James M'Allister, labourer
Alexander M'Alpin, carpenter
Walter M'Alpin, book-binder
Daniel M'Arthur's child
Elizabeth M'Bay

Robert M'Bay
John M'Cabe, hairdresser
Alice M'Cabin's wife
Jenny M'Call
Daniel M'Calla's child
John M'Care
Archibald M'Carey
William M'Carty, soapboiler
David M'Crea
James M'Claskie
Widow M'Clatchee's 2 children
John M'Cleland
John M'Cleuane
Andrew M'Clure
Daniel M'Clia, rope-maker
Alexander M'Cord
Eugenia M'Cordy
Cornelius M'Cormick
Margaret, daughter of Henry M'Cormick
Thomas M'Cormick, merchant
Archibald M'Cowen
John M'Coy
Ann Coy
Jonathan M'Cready
John M'Cready
James M'Creary
Margaret M'Crever.
Catharine M'Croskie
Eleanor M'Croskie, widow
Elizabeth M'Cullen
Sarah M'Curdy.
Deborah M'Curtain
Thomas M'Curtain, school-master, and wife
James M'Cutcheon
Daniel M'Daniel
James M'Daniel, shoemaker
Daniel M'Daniel, aged 80
Martin M'Dermot, grocer
Ann M'Donald, a child
Alexander M'Donald, labourer
Child of Donald M'Donald, painter
Elizabeth M'Donald
James M'Donald, shoemaker
John M'Donald, labourer
John M'Donald's child
Mary M'Donald
William M'Donald, hatter
Hugh M'Dougal, labourer
William M'Dougal, tobacconist
Mrs. M'Dowel

Wm. M'Dowel, tavern-keeper
Wm M'Dowel
Edw. M'Echan, bricklayer, Ir.
Wm. M'Elvee, labourer
John M'Ewing, stone cutter
Enos M'Faden, labourer
James M'Faden's wife
Mary M'Faden
Ann M'Farben
Peter M'Garvey and wife
Edward M'Gechan
Helen M'Gechan and child
Margaret M'Gechan
Mary M'Gee
Edward M'Gill, drayman
Mary M'Gill,
Wm. M'Gill, school-master
Ann M'Ginley, housewife
Philip M'Ginnes's wife
John M'Glathery, a young man
Wm. M'Glochlin
Thomas M'Goldrick
John M'Gontis's child
John M'Gowan
Joseph M'Gowan, carpenter
Wm. M'Gowan
Barney M'Gran, labourer
Daniel M'Grath, porter
John M'Grath
Mich. M'Grath
James M'Graw
John M'Graw, sailor
Barney M'Green
———— M'Griegle
Ann M'Gregor
John M'Gregor's child
Nancy M'Grotty
James M'Guillen
James M'Guire
Mary M'Guire, widow
Peter M'Guire
William M'Guire
John M'Hagan
John M'Illroy
Andrew M'Intire, joiner
Elizabeth M'Intosh
Laughlin M'Intosh
Edward M'Kegan
———— M'Kegan, bricklayer
Anthony M'Kennely
Elizabeth M'Kenzie
Mary M'Kenzie, housewife
Murdock M'Kenzie
John M'Keon

William M'Key, apprentice
Daniel M'ee, sailor
Margaret M'Kigham
Isaac M'Kinby
Hugh M'Kinley
Mrs. M'Kinley
Isaac M'Kinley, hatter
John M'Knall
Alexander M'Lane
Daniel M'Lane
Jane M'Lane
———— M'Lane, a stranger
John M'Lane's wife and two children
Roger M'Lane
William M'Lane, sailor
Ann M'Laughlin
Giles M'Laughlin
John M'Laughlin
John M'Laughlin's wife
John M'Laughlin, merchant
Margaret, M'Laughlin and child
Patrick M'Laughlin's son
William M'Laughlin, labourer
Wm. M'Laughlin, shoemaker
Agnes M'Lean
Elizabeth M'Lane
Jane M'Lean
John M'Lean, inspector
Joseph M'Lean, tailor
Martin M'Lean
Samuel M'Lean, shipwright
Archibald M'Leary, labourer
Joseph M'Lee
Mary M'Lenahan
Angus M'Leod's child
Daniel M'Leod's wife
Dougal M'Leod, labourer
John M'Leod
Malcolm M'Leod, labourer
Mary M'Leod
William M'Leod and daughter
Mary M'Linny
Hugh M'Mann
Philip M'Mannus, blacksmith
James M'Manyman, nailor, and wife
Mary M'Manyman
John M'Manyman
Joseph M'Matlock, carpenter
Mary M'Michael, widow
Catharine M'Mullen
Neil M'Mullen

Francis M'Murren
John M'Nab, shipwright
John M'Nair, clerk
James M'Namara
Gordon M'Neal, sailor
John M'Neal, tailor
Mary M'Neal
John M'Near, apprentice
Felix M'Quid's wife
James M'Quillon, labourer
Sarah M'Rain
Milby M'Raper
Hugh M'Swaine and wife
James Mabey
———— Mack, labourer
Sarah Mack
Elizabeth Madan
John Madan, shoemaker
Patrick Madan's wife
Leonard Madelen
Benjamin Mager, apprentice
Helena Magenis
David Magner, carpenter
Michael Magraw, servant
Francis Major,
John Maitland
John Maloney
Catharine, widow of capt. John
   Molowney
John Mannefield, joiner
Mary Mannefield
Mrs. Mann
William Mann, tailor
Charles Manson
Peter Marclay, cooper
Susannah Mareday, widow
Philip Mareland
Francis Marey
Laurence Marey, perfumer
John Baptiste Maris
John Mark, shopkeeper
Peter Marker, butcher
John Maronee, apprentice
Capt. James Marsh and brother
Curtis Marshal
Francis Marshall, bricklayer
Joseph Marshall, shoemaker
Joseph Marson
Philip Martan
James Martin's son
John Martin, saddler
John Martin's son
Sarah Martin, servant
Judah M'C——
Thos

Abraham C. Mason, merchant
Arabella Mason
John Mason
Joshua Mason, blacksmith
Margaret Mason, Æt. 80
Richard Mason, engine-maker
———— Mass
Samuel Massey
Anne Mastett
J. Masters's wife and 3 children
John Mause's wife and child
Ed. Mathias, wife, & daughter
Elizabeth Maxfield
John Maxfield, labourer
Stephen Maxfield's wife
Margaret Maxwell
Adam May's child
Capt. Mead's wife & daughter
Matthias Meeker, clerk
Gotlieb Meineke, labourer
John Meminger
Gotlieb Menigung, rope-maker
John Mentz, a lad
Ludwig Meo, of Amsterdam
Mary Mercer, widow
Joseph Mercier, and wife Ann
John Merck, store-keeper
Peter Merchel, butcher
Evan Meredith's wife Susannah
Samuel Merian, merchant
Jos. Merson, bridle-bit-cutter
Peter Merson
Miles Mervin, school-master, &
   wife
John Mesner's wife
Barbara Mettelbury
Adam Meyers's daughter
Henry Meyers's apprentice
John Meyers's child
Peter Meyer, carter, and wife
Sebastian Meyer, baker
Thomas Meyer's wife, & daug.
Peter Miercken, sugar-refiner,
———— Miers, wife and servant
Sarah Middleton, sen. widow
Sarah Middleton, jun. spinster
Sarah Mifflin ⎱ children of
Hester Mifflin ⎰   Charles
Thomas Miller's son Joseph
Andreas Miller's child
Anne Miller
Arthur Miller's child
Catharine Miller, widow
Charles Miller
         Miller, porter

Chrifto. Miller, brufh-maker
Dorothy Miller
George Miller, labourer
Hannah Miller
Henry Miller
James Miller's wife and two
 children
John Miller and child
Captain John Miller's widow
John Miller, carpenter
John Miller, carter
John Miller, clerk
John Miller, labourer
Ifaac Miller, merchant
Margaret Miller
Mary Miller
Michael Miller, fen. fhoemaker
Michael Miller's daughter
Richard Miller, ftudent of law
Sufannah Miller
Widow Miller
William Miller, fhoe-maker
Wife and child of Mr. Miller,
 rigger
Mary Millington
Philip Milligan's wife
Elizabeth Mills
Thomas Mills
Walter Mills, fhoemaker
Edward Milner's wife & fervant
Chriftian Minehart, fugar-baker
William Miner, fervant
William Minor
Charles Minfter, labourer
John Mintz
Elizabeth Mifcamp
Elizabeth Mitchell
Jacob Mitchell's child
Mary Mitchell
Mary Mittinton
Veronia Mittman
Jacob Mirwan, and 3 children
William Modick's child
James Moffat, tailor
Rebecca Moffat
Rob't Moffat, waterman, wife
 and child
Catharine Molliner
George Moir
James Mollineux, and daugh.
John Mollineux's 2 children
Francis Monday
John Monday
Mary Monday

Elizabeth Montgomery
Child of John Montgomery,
 weaver
John Montgomery's 3 children
Dorothy Mood
Robert Moody, bricklayer
Mary Mooney
Ann Moore
Caroline, daughter of Thomas
 L. Moore
David Moore
Fanny Moore, fervant, Germ
George Moore
Major James Moore, livery-fta-
 ble-keeper
Jane Moore
John Moore, painter, and child
Samuel Moore, blackfmith
Thomas Moore's child
Widow Moore
Wm. Moore and two children
John Moore
Jofeph Mordeck, labourer
Eleanor Morgan, wafherwoman
Hannah Morgan
Jacob Morgan, merchant
John Morgan, jun.
John Morgan's child
Mary Morgan
Robert Morphet
Ann Morris
Anthony P. Morris, china-mer-
 chant
Brooke Morris
George Morris, gardener
John Morris, clerk
John Morris, phyfician, and
 wife
John Morris's child
Luke Morris, Æt. 87
Martha Morris
Mary Morris
Richard B. Morris
Samuel W. Morris, apprentice
Samuel Morris, cooper
William Morris
Alexander Morifon, ftorekeeper
John Morifon, copper-fmith
Wife and child of John Morri-
 fon, labourer
John Morifon's daughter
Ifabella Morifon
Mary Morifon's child
—— Morifon, labourer, Scotl.

Widow Morrison's child
William Morrison
John Morrow, jun. gunsmith
Mrs. ——— Morrow
Rosina Morrow
Alexander Mortimer, gardener
Deborah Morton
John Morron and apprentice
Christian Moser
Mary Moss
Marquis Monbrun   -
Philip Mountree, brewer
Wife of Nicholas Muff, harness-maker
Ann Mullen, mantua-maker
Catharine Mullen
Edward Mullen
James Mullen, hatter
James Mullen's wife
John Mullen, chairmaker
Mary Mullen
Michael Mullen's two children
Patrick Mullen
Robert Mullen, house-carpenter, and apprentice
James Mullener, apprentice
Edmund Mullery, grocer
James Mumford, blacksmith
Major Henry Mumford
Rachel Mumford
Child of Robert Murdoch, labourer
Sarah Murdoch
——— Murley
Ann Murphy
John Murphy, black-smith
Mary Murphy
Michael Murphy's daughter
Richard Murphy
Susannah Murphy
Timothy Murphy
Margaret Murthwaite
Mary Murthwaite
Rev. Alexander Murray, D. D.
Eleanor Murray
James Murray, shoemaker, Ir.
Robert Murray's wife and child
Sarah Murray
William Murray
Mrs. ——— Musketts
Rebecca Musgrove, a stranger
Widow Musterholt
Adam Myers, baker
Catharine Myers

Hannah Myers, servant
Margaret Myers
Henry Myers, hair-dresser
John Myers's child
Margaret Myers
Michael Myers
Michael Mynick
Sophia Mynick
Adam Myon, labourer
John Myrietta
Jac. Mytinger, tavern-keeper, and wife
Henry Nagle's mother-in-law
Mary Nagle
Hannah Nailor
John Nailor
Samuel Napp
William Nash, baker
Lewis Nass, blacksmith
——— Navarre
Thomas Nave's wife
Thomas Near
Israel Nedham, skinner, Engl.
Robert Neeley, sailor
Tho. Neeves, carpenter, & wife
Margaret Neil
Wife and girl of Andrew Nielson, tavern-keeper
George Niess, shoemaker
Benedict Nesmos, son, & daugh.
Elizabeth Neman
Thomas Nemerson
Timmons Nevil
Elizabeth New
Anthony Newingham
John Newling, a lad
Elizabeth Newman
Fred. Newman's wife & child
Susannah Newman
Forbes Newton's wife
Margaret Nibley
Magnus Nice, oyster-man
Martha Nichols, spinster, Æt. 70
Wm. Nichols, Æt. 73
Mary Nichols, wife of ditto
Wm. Nichols, wheelwright, and wife
Thomas Nicholson, joiner
John Nick
Augustus Niel
Jane, daughter of Wm. Niles
Elizabeth Noble
Catharine Nodler
Anthony Noll, ropemaker

Fred. Noltenius, school-master
Cathar. Norley, wash-woman
Joseph Norman's wife
Wife of Adam Norris, huckster
Abigail North
Colonel North's wife
Joseph North's child
George Norton's child
Sarah Norton, servant
Sarah Norton, widow
Francis Nugne
Wm. Nunn
Christi a na Oatenheimer, Germ.
Peter Oatenheimer's wife, Ger.
Phil. Oatenheimer's wife, Germ.
Daniel Offley, anchor-smith
Bridget O'Bryant, Ir.
James O'Bryant, carpenter, Ir.
Dennis O'Connel
John O'Dare
John O'Donald
Mary O'Donald
———— O'Dolph, a butcher
Charles Ogden's wife
Joseph Ogilby's wife
Edward O'Hara, clerk
Elizabeth O'Hara, housewife
Thomas O'Hara, clerk
Ann Oiler, Æt. 77
Cornelius O'Leary
Humphrey O'Leary
Henry O'Niel, labourer, Ir.
Catharine O'Niel
John Onger's wife
Edward Orange, blacksmith
Michael O'Rourke's wife
Robert Orr, Ir.
Wife of Nich. Otway, nailor, Ir.
John Osborn
Wm. Osborn, steward to the
  President
Hannah Osgood
Sarah A. Otis
Thomas Owner, carpenter
George Pack
Hannah Packman
Wife of John Packworth, shoe-
  maker, Eng.
———— Page's child
William Paine
Jacob Painter, apprentice
Charles Palmer, house car-
  penter, and his two sisters,
  viz. Tacy Palmer, and
R

Aaron Palmer's child
Elihu Palmer's wife
Hannah, wife of Samuel Palmer
Penelope Palmer
Samuel Palmer, ship-wright
Thomas Palmer, shipwright
Thomas Palmer's two children
Sarah Palling
Martha Pallock
William Parham's wife & child
Wm. Parham, jun. carpenter,
John Park
Ann Parker, servant
George Parker
John Parker, shoe-maker
John Parker, carpenter, and
  child, Ir.
Joseph Pilmore Parker
Mat. Parker, tailor, and wife
Wife of Samuel Parker, brass-
  founder
John Parkhill
Honora Parkinson
Eleanor Parks
James Park's wife
John-Park's brother
Mary Parks
Wife of Matthias Parks, linen-
  draper
Edward, and Isaac Parrish, jun.
  sons of Isaac Parrish, hatter
John Parkill, whitesmith, Ir.
Daniel Parvin
Catharine Patch and child
John Patch
Andrew Patterson, carpenter
Edward Patterson
Richard Patterson
Sarah Patterson
Samuel Patterson's child
Jas. Pattison, student of physic
Robert Patton, bookbinder
George Paul, tailor
Peter Paul's son
Robert Paul's wife
Sydney Paul, widow
John Pea
James Peale's two children
James Pearce
John Pearce
Jos. Pearson, heelmaker, & wife
Widow of Wm. Pearson
Sarah Pearce

Joseph Peddrick's son
Mary Peifter
Vincent M. Pelofi, merchant
Samuel Pemberton and child
Doctor John Penington
Mary Penington, a child
Alexander Penman, coachmaker
Mary Penny
John Pennycook, apprentice
Amos Penquoite
Phœbe Penquoite
Jemima Penrofe, fervant
Hannah Penton
Ifaac Penton, farmer, and wife
Samuel Penn, baker
Jofeph Pennel
Ann Pepper
Mary Pepper, layer out of the
dead
Foulard Perdue's daughter
Mary Perdue
Sarah Perkins
Mary Perry's child
Wm. Perry
——— Perry, fhoemaker, Ir.
Jac. Peters, baker, & wife Sarah
John Peters, fen. bifcuit-haker
John Peters. junior, tutor
Philip Peters, diftiller, & wife
Ruth Peters
Thomas Pew
Charlotte Petit
Edward Peyton's wife
Stephen Peyton's child
Son of John Pheiffer, cooper
Wm. Phager, tailor
Dr. Fred. Phile, naval-officer
Jeremiah Philemon, barber
Widow Philemon
Andrew Philips's child
Geo. A. Philips, & fon, merchant
——— Philips
Mrs. Philips
PhilipPhile, mufician
John Phyfick porter
James Pickering, fhoemaker
James Pickering, tailor
James Pickering, ftore-keeper
Son of Timothy Pickering
Chriftian Pierce, cooper
James Pierce, coach maker
John Pierce, fhip-carpenter,
and wife

John Pierce's daughter Anne
——— Piercy, potter, and fon
John Pircy, apprentice
Mary Piercy, apprentice
——— Pierre, 2 of the fame
name, bakers
Mary Pierfon
Anne Pigot
Lewis Pignol, clerk
Benjamin Pike, and wife
James Pike
John Pilliger, cooper
Charles Pine, ftocking weaver
Eleanor Piper
George Piper, tailor, and wife,
John Piper, cooper
Benjamin Pitfield
Anna Plaff
Jeremiah Plan
John Plankinhorn, labourer
Henry Plates, baker, Germ.
Jacob Plucker and child
Barbara Poagnet
Hen. Petterman's fifter-in-law
Sarah Pollard
Catharine Poop, Germ.
Mary Poor
George Pope
Margaret Porkenbine, Eliza.
her daughter, and a child
Philip Port, labourer
Charles Porter
John Porter's fon and daugh-
ter, and two fervant girls
Rich. Porter, tallow-chandler
Thomas Porter, labourer
Andrew Pottenftein's wife
Mrs. ——— Potter
Edmond, fon of Edmond Potter
Mary Potts
Benjamin Poultney, merchant,
wife and daughter
Elizabeth Poule
Samuel Powel, fpeaker of the
fenate, and fervant
Francis Powers, labourer, Ger.
Ifaac Powerfhon
Mr. Prifflet
——— Pragers, merchant
Henry Pratt, wife, and child
James Pratt's wife
Mary Pratt

John Preal
Barbara Preston, Germ.
Wife and 3 children of Wm.
  Preston, brush-maker
John Price
Teney Price
Thomas Price
Robert Priestley, whitesmith
Susannah Prince, spinster
Stephen Prisling
Isabella Provost
Joseph Pruett, tailor
Thomas Pugh
Francis Pugsley
John Puracier
Mary Purde
George Purdy, tailor
Wm. Purvis's wife
Wm. Pusey's daughter Eliza.
Qua, a negro
Phillis Quando
Catharine Quigley
James Quigly, carpenter, and
  child
John Quilman, servant
Gascoigne Raby and wife
Rachel, a black girl
Christian Bach's daughter
Geo. C. Rainholdt & daughter
John Rain's child
George Rainsford
Christopher Rakestraw
Sarah Rakestraw's child
Cathaine Ralph's child
William Ralston, merchant, and
  son John
Mr. Ralston
Thomas Rambaut, carpenter
Child of Archibald Randall,
  ship-carpenter
Thomas Randall's child
John Randolph, tobacconist
Ann Rankin
Elizabeth Rankin
Jo   Rankin
Margaret Rankin
Hannah Rapp
Eliza Rarich, widow, and daugh-
  ter Sarah
Sarah Razor, Æt. 22
John Ratler, porter
Elizabeth Rauch

Jacob Ravalie, labourer
John Reach's widow
Jo   Ready
Michael Ready
Maria Read
John Reap, shoemaker
Jonathan Reas
Jacob Reckther, labourer
Sarah Reddick
Francis Redman's wife, and a
  lodger, name unknown
Jacob Reece, jun.
Mary Reece
John Reedle, tailor, and daugh.
  ter Sarah
Casper Reel, baker
Edward Rees, joiner
Jacob Rees's wife, daughter &
  son
Mr. Reffeit's child
George Reh
Alexander Reid
Andrew Reid, bricklayer
Ann Reid
George Reid and wife
Henry Reid, merchant
James Reid, silk-dyer
James Reid, Æt. 75, and daugh.
  ter Sarah
Margaret Reid
Mary Reid
Rebecca Reid, widow
Samuel Reid's wife
William Reid's child
John Reidy's child
James Reily, servant
Maria Reily
George Reigner, tobacconist
Widow Reigner, his mother
George Reily
John Reinick, brickmaker
John Reinick, baker
Lewis Reisele, butcher
George Reser
Nancy Reiter
Jacob Relchner
John Reller
Joannes Relwiez
Afelae Remer
Anthony Renard
Jane Renny
—— Renvalt
Widow Resle

Chriftian Reting's child
Chriftian Rettig
Ludwig Reuth's wife
Adam Revely
George Rex
Chriftopher Rexrold, apprentice
James Reynolds's wife
John Reynolds
Mary Reynolds
Jofeph Ribaux's child
Catharine Rice
George Rice's child
John Rice, labourer
Lawrence Rice
William Rice
Charlotte Richards
Daniel Richards, lumber-merchant
Daniel Richards's fon
Eliza Richards
John Richards
Mrs. ——Richards
William Richards, butcher
Samuel Richards's wife
Steel Richards, fhoemaker
Barbara Richardfon, houfe-wife
Barnabas Richardfon
Elizabeth Richardfon
George Richardfon's wife
John Richardfon
Jofeph Richardfon, jun.
Lucy Richardfon
Rebecca Richardfon
Thomas Richardfon
William Richardfon's child
George Richner, tobacconift
Gotlieb Richter, labourer
Jacob Richter
George Riddle
James Riddle and wife
John Ridge, jun.
Mary Ridge, milliner
John Ridgway
Frederic Reib, wheelwright
John Rieb
Leonard Riebfher's child
Cafper Riehl, labourer
John Riehl's daughter
George Rife's child
George Riley, baker
Mary Riley
Jacob Rilt, fhoemaker
John Rilvit, fawyer

Frederic Rine, labourer
James Ringland
George Rinhard
Conrad Rink, fhoemaker
Elizabeth Riply
Mary Riply
Alexander Ritchie's wife
John Ritchie
Mary Ritchie
Mr. —— Rutter's daughter
John Roach's wife & 2 children
Morris Roach, hoftler
John Robeau
Jacob Roberdeau, printer
Robert ——, a failor
Aaron Roberts
Ann Roberts
Charles Roberts
Mrs. —— Roberts, houfe-wife
Oliver Roberts
Rebecca Roberts
Robert Roberts, late of Merion
Thomas Roberts, labourer
Thomas Roberts, filverfmith
William Roberts
Jofeph Robertfon, carpenter
Lætitia, daughter of Daniel Robins
Sufannah Robins
Abraham Robinfon
James Robinfon, carpenter, Ir.
James Robinfon's child
Jane Robinfon, widow
John Robinfon, blackfmith
John C. Robinfon's fervant
Jofeph Robinfon
Judge Robinfon's young man
Mary Robinfon
Robert Robinfon, fhoemaker
Sarah Robinfon
Thomas Robinfon, weaver
William Robinfon, bricklayer
—— Rochbaud, Fr.
Mary Rock
Jacob Rodell
Elizabeth Roderfield, widow
Philip Roderfield
Nicholas Roderwalter's daugh.
Sarah Rodman, of R. Ifland
Benjamin Rogers's child
Gilbert Rogers, and child
John Rogers, corder
Margaret Rogers
Wife of the rev. Wm. Rogers

John Rohr's daughter
John Roman, currier
Elizabeth Roney, ſervant
Magdalen Roone
Suſannah Roring
Hugh Roſs, blackſmith, wife,
  and ſon
John Roſs
Wm. Roſt, ſhoemaker
Mary Rotherwalter
Jacob Rix Rott, a lad
Roſina Rott, a ſervant
Henry Rouris's daughter
Elizabeth Ronſh
James Rowan, ſtore-keeper
John Rowe, carpenter
John Rowe
Barbara Ruber
Catharine Ruckhard
John Rudolph
John Rugan's daughter
John Rugers's
Frederie Ruhl's ſon
George Ruhl's ſon
John Ruleford, labourer
Jacob Rump's child
Roſina Runkel
Leonard Ruſh, ſhoemaker
Mary Ruſh, widow
Wm. Ruſh's child
Thomas Ruſſel, ſailor
Leonard Ruſt, tailor
Wm. Rutherford
Jacob Rutter
Margaret Rutter
Samuel Rutter's 2 children
Lucy Ryan
Mr. ——— Ryan
Saberne, Fr.
5 Sailors, (names unknown)
Abraham Salter
Iſaac Samms
Sampſon ———, a negro man
Mary Sampſon
John Sanders, button maker
Sarah, a young woman
John Sattersfield's wife
Elizabeth Saub
Frederic Sauber
——— Saubier's wife
Robert Saubiers, blackſmith
Philip Sauerman, ſhoemaker,
  and wife

Jacob Sawyer, baker
Wife and daughter of dr. Ben-
  jamin Say
Leonard Sayer's wife
Matthias Saylor, painter, wife,
  and ſiſter
John Scantling, porter
Jonathan Scantling
Mary Schaff
Adam Schaffer, labourer
George Schaffer, cooper
Jacob Schaffer
Widow Scheiffells
Chriſtiana Schieff's girl
George Schmidt
George Schmidt's child
Henry Schmidt, and wife
Jo   Schmidt
Margaret Schmidt
George Schneider, carpenter
John Schreier, and wife
Frederic Schreiner's daughter
John Schreminger
Ann Schrider
John Schrieck
John Schrier, ſhoemaker, and
  wife
Martin Schrier
Thomas Schriever, blackſmith
John Schultz, labourer
John Schwaab, ſhoemaker
Lawrence Schwaab, ſhoemaker
Adam Schwaadt
Captain Schwartz, Denmark
Elizabeth Sclader
Aaron Scott
Andrew Scott
Ann Scott
Benjamin Scott
Henry Scott, labourer, & wife
John Scott, tailor, and wife
Margaret Scott
Mary Scott
——— Scott, clerk
Joſeph Scull
Frederick Seaford, joiner
Francis Seamore
Chriſto. Search, wheelwright
Jacob Sears, blackſmith, and
  child
David Seaven
Martin Seebole, ſchool-maſter

Paulus Seegift, weaver
Henry Seen's child
Jacob Seger, baker
Jacob Seiffer's daughter
—— Sein's wife
Michael Seip, tailor
Widow Seitz's daughter
James Sekwire
Jacob Seller, tailor, and wife
Joseph Sellers, watch-maker, Wm.&Susanna, sons & daughter of Wm. Sellers, printer
Wife of Henry Semler, shoemaker
Jona. D. Sergeant, attorney
—— Sergeois
Francis Serres, stay-maker, Fr.
Wife of Benja. Servant, sailor
7 Servants, (names unknown)
Isabella Service
Ann Sewell
Catharine Sexton
Conrard Seybert's wife
Christiana Seyfert
Elizabeth Shabby, widow
Widow Shaff's child
Adam Shaffer, porter
Barny Shaffer's child
Francis Shaffner's wife
John Shakespeare
Martha Shakespeare
Stephen Shakespeare, weaver
Dorothy Shall
Bernard Shamo's wife
James Shankling
Henry Shara
Anthony Sharp, tailor
John Sharp's child
John Sharp, and daughter
Nehemiah Sharp, tailor
Mr.—— Shaestocker
Henry Shaw, and wife
Henry- Shaw ware-house man
Henry Shawster's daughter
Henrick Shear, tailor
Elizabeth Shearman
John Shearwood
Daniel Sheegan
Henry Sheerer
Wm. Sheets, labourer
Adam Shellbecker, shoemaker
Frederic Sheller, blacksmith
Jacob Sheniger

George Shepherd
Jacob Shepherd's child
Robert Shepherd, shop-keeper
Wilhelmina, daughter of Wm. Sheperd
John Sherh, baker
Elizabeth Sherman
Abraham Sheridan's child
Wm. Sheridan, & daughter
John Sherwood, carpenter, and wife
Sallows Shewell's wife
Juliana Shewelly, widow
James Shillingsford
Richard Shilly, hatter
Christian Shemblers wife
Jacob Shiney
Margaret Shingle
Amos Shingleton
Bernard Shiphar's wife
Wm. Shipley, grazier
Rebecca Shipping
John Shippey, musician, and child
Matthias Shiltz's sister
Frederic Shneider, stone-cutter and son
Elizabeth Shocker
George Shocker, and child
Jacob Shocker, labourer
Matthias Shocker, & mother
Amos Shoemaker
Jonathan Shoemaker, cabinet-maker
Joseph Shoemaker
Mary Shoemaker
Michael Shoemaker, livery-stabler
Samuel Shoemaker, jun. carpenter, from Cheltingham.
Henry Sheffield
Adam Shordy
—— Shore, widow
Christopher Short
Mrs. —— Short
Matthew Short's child
Henry Shreader
Martin Shriar
John Shriber, butcher
Thomas Shriber
Henry Shrider, baker & wife
Jacob Shrince, comb-maker

Chriftopher Shriner, tutor, and
  wife Elizabeth
Jacob Shriner,
Jacob Shriner, jun. fkinner
Nicholas Shriner, fkinner
Philip Shrite, ftocking-weaver
Elizabeth Shubart
Jacob Shubart, blackfmith
Jacob Shubert, labourer
Michael Shubart, diftiller, fon,
  and daughter
Sarah Shubart
Widow Shuber
John Shute, baker
George Sibbald's child
Baptifte Sicard
Sarah Sickel
Catharine Sickfon
Adam Sifert
Cafper Silver, wheelwright, and
  wife
Jofeph Silves
Mrs. —— Simmonds
John Simmonds's child
Wife of John Simmonds, tailor
John Simpfon
Mary Simpfon, widow
Samuel Simpfon
John Sims
Wooddrop Sims, merchant
Elizabeth Singer, widow
Thomas Singleton's child
George Sink's child
John Siper
Charles Sitz and fervant girl
Elizabeth Sitz
Henry Skeffold, apprentice
Richard Skelly
Rachel Skinner, and daughter
  Mary
David Slack
Mifs Slack
William Slade, ftore-keeper
Abraham Slater, currier, Eng.
Gotlieb Slater's child
Henrietta Slater
MichaelSleefman's fervant-man
Frederick Slicker
Widow Slint's fon
Andrew Smith, labourer
Ann Smith
Barbara Smith

Benjamin Smith, merchant, of
  Burlington
Catharine Smith
Charles Smith's child
Conrad Smith, farmer, Germ.
Dr. Smith's wife
Elizabeth Smith
George Smith, potter, & child
Wife of Henry Smith, carpenter
Henry Smith, labourer, & wife
James L. Smith, factor of cards
James Smith, merchant
James Smith
Jane Smith and child
Jeffe Smith and child
John Smith, fen. merchant, his
  fon John, & daughter Sarah
John Smith, chair-maker
John Smith, cabinet-maker
John Smith, labourer, and child
John Smith, fhoemaker
Lewis Smith
Margaret Smith, houfe-wife
Mary Smith
Matthew Smith, painter
Nathan Smith's fon
Rebecca Smith
Thomas Smith, commiffioner of
  loans
Thomas Smith, bricklayer, Ir.
Widow Smith
William Smith
Child of William Smith, fea-
  captain
Charles Smithfield, tutor
John Smithfon, Ir.
George Snellbecker
James Snouder
Leonard Snouder's mother
Anna Maria Snyder
Anthony Snyder and fon
Charles Snyder's wife
Chriftian Snyder, farmer
Gulfer Snyder
Frederic Snyder, fergeant at
  arms to the fenate of Penn-
  fylvania, and his fon George
George Snyder, baker
Philip Snyder, coachmaker
Henry Soden
Guftavus Soderftrom, fea-cap-
  tain
Ann Solander

John Sommervell, weaver, Ir.
John and Isabella Sommervell,
children of John Sommervell,
cabinet-maker
Elizabeth Sooks
Philip Sorter
Robert Sorter
Robert Sowerbee, balckfmith
Philip Sowerman and wife
John Spalder, plaifterer
Widow Spatzen
Townfend Speakman, apothe-
cary
George Speel's daughter
Henry Speel, baker, wife, fer-
vant man, and woman
Widow Speel
Widow Speers
Eve Spence, fervant
George Spigle's wife
Charles Spinley
Sophia Spitzburgh
Sophia Splitfpike
Margaret Spotts, Germ.
Rev. James Sproat, D. D.
Major Sproat and wife
Nancy Sproat
York Sprogel
Andrew Sprowl
Margaret Sprowl
Hefter Squirnel, Æt. 82
Richard Stack, bricklayer
Peter Stackard's wife
Benjamin Stackhoufe
Sufannah Stackhoufe
Thomas Stackhoufe
Hannah Staggs
Joanna, wife of John Stair
John Stall, ftndent of medicine
Jofeph Stanbury's fon
William Stancape
Lucas Stanch
James Stanford, fhoemaker
William Stanker, tailor
Margaret, wife of Laurence
Stantz
George Star and child
Rachel, Lydia, and Sarah,
daughters of James Starr,
fhoemaker
William Starkley, labourer,
wife, and child
William Starrat

Frederic William Starrman,
merchant, and apprentice
William Statton, hatter
William St. Clair
James Steel
John Steel, carpenter, and two
children
John Steel, tavernkeeper
——Steel, cooper, wife, father,
and daughter
Mary Steel
Stephen Steel's child
Widow Steel's daughter
William Steel, fhoemaker
Frederic Steelman, tailor, and
wife
William Stein, clerk
James Steiner, ftorekeeper
Nicholas Steiner, labourer
Cafper Steinmitz
John Steinmitz, cooper, and
Mary, his mother
Peter Stenhyfter, laft-maker
Andrew Stenton, a child
Daniel Stephens, fervant, Ir.
Fanny Stephens
John Stephens, fadler
Mrs. Stephens and daughter
Aftrfield Stephenfon
James Stephenfon
John Stephenfon
Mrs. Stephenfon's daughter
Catharine Sternkarl, fervant,
Germ.
David Stewart, clerk
James Stewart
John Stewart's daughter
Ifaac Stewart
Samuel Stewart, tailor
William Stewart, bookbinder,
Edinburgh
Wife of Henry Stiles, merchant
William Stiles, jun. merchant
William Stiles, fen ftonecutter,
wife, and fon William, Eng.
Ifaac Still, tailor
Mary Still, fervant
John Stillas, watchmaker
George Stiller, fhoemaker
John Stillie, watchman
John Stillwaggon, hatter
Ifaac Stine's child

Captain Sting
James Stinton, servant
Laurence Stintz's widow
William Stirrets, blacksmith
George Stocks, hair-dresser and child
John Stocks, jun.
—— Stocker's child
Ebenezer Stokes, silver-smith, Eng.
Elizabeth Stokes, widow
George Stokes and wife
James Stokes's son
John Stokes, bottler
Richard Stokes's child
John Stoltz, baker
William Stone, merchant
Luke Storch
Jonathan Stormitz
James Stinfen, servant, Ir.
Ebenezer Stotts, apprentice
Catharine Stouble
Peter Stounhoufer, servant
George Stow, turner
Hannah Stow
John Stow's widow
Peter Stoy's daughter
John Stranger
Hannah Stratton, a child
John Stratton, labourer
Peter Streecheifer
James Stretcher's wife and child
John Stricker, clerk
—— Stritten, lace-weaver
Paul Stromfeltz, mealman, and wife, Germ.
Captain Strong's daughter
Lætitia Stroud's child
William Stroud, plaifterer
Child of mr. Strutton, rigger
Andrew Stuart's child
Adam Stubert, clerk
George Stubert, apprentice
Hefter Stubert, spinfter
Jacob Stubert, labourer
Daniel Stubbs, carter
Peter Stuckard, carpenter, wife and child
William Stutt, cooper, and wife
Martha Stutzer
Anthony Suay
Chriftian Sulger, baker

David Sullivan, ftorekeeper
Laura Sullivan
Catharine Summers
Edward Summers
Elizabeth Summers
—— Summers, a young man, from Carolina
Francis Summers
Peter Summers, wife and three children
Jac. Sunnock, labourer, Germ.
John Sunnock, trunk-maker and apprentice
Simon Sunnock's wife
Sufannah Supple
Charles Surtz, currier, and child
John Sutherland, merchant
Emon Sutt, keeper of a boarding houfe
Mary-Sutton
Samuel Swaine
William Swaine
Mrs. Swaine
Laurence Swall's wife
Jofeph Swanfon's wife
Jo Swanwick, fhip-carpenter
Margaret Swanwick
Chriftiana Swartz, and two children
George Swartz, carpenter
Peter Swartz's fon
Ann Sweeny
Edward Sweeny, labourer, and child, Ir.
John Sweeny's child
Morgan Sweeny, wife, and child
Jacob Swin
Mary Swin
Hugh Swine and wife
John Swoope
Penelope Sword
Edward Swordan
George Sydes
Elizabeth Sykes
Mary Sykes, Æt. 15
John Syler
Cafper Sylvius, wheelwright
Widow Sylvins
Charles Syng, weigh-mafter and wife
Mr. Tacker
David Taggart, carpenter.

Sarah Taggart
Thomas Taggart
William Taggart
Elizabeth Tannenberg, sen.
Elizabeth Tannenberg, jun.
Sarah Tarcen
Robert Tate, merchant, Scot.
Joseph Tatem, tailor
Eleanor Taye
Hannah Taye
Abigail Taylor, widow
Elizabeth Taylor and child
George Taylor
Isaac Taylor, ironseller, wife
   and sister Sarah
Margaret Taylor, servant
Richard Taylor's child
Robert Taylor's wife and child
Robert Taylor, clerk
Samuel Taylor, brush-maker,
   and his daughter Mary
Temperance Taylor
Thomas Taylor
Thomas Taylor's child
William Taylor's wife
————— Teeny, a young man
John Teim, hair-dresser
A. Teiffler
William Teirnan
Andrew Ten-Eyck
Helen Terence
Henry Test, hatter
John Teteres
William Tharp, merchant
John Thatcher's child
Benjamin Thaw, jun.
Maria Thaw
Enoch Thomas, bricklayer, and
   three children
Hannah Thomas
James Thomas, ship-carpenter
John Thomas, tailor
John Thomas, clerk
Lewis Thomas, carter, & wife
Margaret Thomas
Mary Thomas
Richard Thomas, brass-founder
   and wife
Richard Thomas, labourer and
   wife
Robert Thomas's wife
Zachariah Thomas

Adam Thompson, a young lad
Elizabeth Thompson
Jacob Thompson's child
John Thompson's wife
John Thompson, labourer
Sarah Thompson
Thomas Thompson's daughter
   Jane, and son John
Andrew Thomson, blacksmith
David Thomson, shoemaker
Wife of James Thomson, inn-
   keeper, at the Indian Queen
Margaret Thomson, Ir.
Mary Thomson
Peter Thomson, sen. scrivener
Zaccheus Thorn, hatter, and
   wife
Thomas Thornelly, jun.
Wife of John Thornhill, shoe-
   maker
Jos. Thornhill, house-carpenter
Nicholas Thornman's child
George Thornton, currier
Mary Thornton
Jacob Thumb, plumber, and Su-
   sannah, his daughter
John Thumb's child
Jacob Tice
Paul Tiggitz
Jacob Till
Frederick Tillman, tailor
Dean Timmons, tavern-keeper
William Timmons, apprentice
Timothy, a black man
Richard Tinker, drayman
Richard Tittermary's wife
Jacob Titty
Elizabeth Titwood
Peter Tobo
Jacob Tobyn's wife
John Todd, sen. teacher, and
   wife
John Todd, jun. attorney at
   law
George Togle, shoemaker
Ann Tollman
Tom, a negro
Jacob Tomkins, jun. merchant
Bartholomew Tool, storekeeper
Charlotte Tool
Thomas Topliff, grocer
——— Tourette, France

John Town
Mary Town
Richard Town
Henry Townfend, a child
Thomas Townfend, Æt. 69
Peter Trabar
Nancy Tracy
Nelly Trades
Walter Traquair, ftone-cutter
Elizabeth Traveller
Henry Traveller, blackfmith
Frederick Traven, labourer
Elizabeth Traverfe
Martha Trefs
Michael Trinker's man-fervant
Fred. Trott's daughter Mary
Daniel Trotter's child
William Trotter's wife
Wm. Truckenmiller, tobacconift
Richard Trufs, joiner
Ann Trufter
Richard Trufter
Jacob Tryon, tinman
Arabella Tudor
Major Tudor's two daughters
Sarah Tureau
Mary Turner
Peter Turner
William Turner, baker
Anthony Turret
Elizabeth Tyfon
William Ubert
Jacob Udree, tavern-keeper
Chriftian Uhler
Jacob Ultree, merchant
Henry Unis
Peter Uttenberger
George Utts, labourer, & wife
——— Uvis
Child of William Valentine
Matthew Vandegrift
John Vanderflyce's boy
Ferdinand Vandigla, fhoemaker
John Vandufer, blackfmith, & child
Adam Vanhorne, tailor
Jerem'. Vanhorne, board-merchant
Mr. ——— Vanier's child
Hannah Vanludner
Sarah Vanfe
Wm. Vannemond's child
Mr. ——— Vanfickle

James Vanuxem's child
Captain Van Voorhis's child
Andrew Vanweller's wife
John Vanummell
Adam Vafs's two children
Elizabeth Vafs
Captain John Vehall
Jane Vent
Conrad Verglafs, tailor
John B. Vernies
Mary Veffie
Laurence Veft's wife
John Vettar
Peter Vickar
Elizabeth Vickerly
Lætitia Vickey, mantua-maker
Phi. Vidfell, band box-maker, and wife
Charlotte Viempft
Matthew Viempft
Henry Vierheller, fawyer and child
Mrs. ——— Villet
Chriftian Villiporey's fon
Jacob Vinckler's wife
Violet, a black girl
Frederick Vogel's wife and daughter
Gotlich Vogel's daughter
Jacob Volker
Catharine Vonweiller
Elizabeth Wack
Godfrey Wackfel
G. Wachfmuth's maid
James Waddle
Thomas Wade
Catharine Wadman
William Wager
Ann Wagner
Chriftopher Wagner, tailor
John Wagner
Widow Wagner
Peter Wagner's wife, & fifter
Abraham Walders, gunfmith, and child
Andrew Waldrick's child
John Wales, and wife
Andrew Walker's fon
Alexander Walker, and fon
Edward Walker, merchant, of Birmingham
Emanuel Walker, merchant, wife, and fon John

James Walker, a child
Matthew Walker, clerk
Ralph Walker's wife
Richard Walker, labourer
Robert Walker
Samuel Walker's wife Eliza.
William Walker
William Wall, servant
Robert Wallace, jun.
John Wallis, hatter
Rebecca Wallis
Richard Waln's child
Aaron Walton
Abraham Walton, blacksmith
Captain Walters and daughter
Catharine Walters, and child
Charles Walters, labourer
George Walters, wife & daugh.
Jacob Walters, a child
Jacob Walters's wife
Jeremiah Walters, mason
Peter Walters, shoemaker
Mary Walton
Samuel Walton's daugh. Sarah
Poblick Calvelt Wanelcan
George War's son
Valentine War, chair-maker
Jeremiah Ward
Benjamin Ware, turner
Wm. Waring, mathematician
John Warmington
Teny Warn
Alice, wife of Swen Warner
Ephraim Warner, apprentice
Hezekiah Warner
Jane Warner, widow
John Warner, clerk
Mary Warner
Magdalene Warner
Wm. Warnick's wife & child
Wm. Warnick, jun.
John Warren
Isaac Warren, sawyer, wife, and son
Wm. Warren, blacksmith, and child
Wm. Warren, sailor
Michael Wartman
Warner Washington, student of medicine
Christopher Wassom, watchman, and child Elizabeth
Widow Wassom's daughter

James Watkins, joiner
Benjamin Watson
Wife, and child, of Charles C. Watson, tailor
Elizabeth Watson
Mary Watson
Robert Watson, labourer, and son
Wife of Samuel Watson's coppersmith
Thomas Watter's daughter
Ignatius Watteman's wife
John Watters's child
Wife of Nathan Watters, hatter
Beulah Watters
Margaret Watts
James Watts
Henry Wayland, weaver
Jane Wayland
Henry Wealler
Samuel Weatherby, corder, & wife
Thomas Weatherby ⎫
Samuel Weatherby ⎬ sons of
Joseph Weatherby ⎬ ditto
Benja. Weatherby ⎭
Adam Weaver, brick-maker
Andrew Weaver, tailor
George Weaver, and daughter
Jacob Weaver, and 2 children
Wife of John Weaver, painter
Nathaniel Weaver
Widow Weaver, and child
Eleanor Webb
Elizabeth Webb, widow
Simon Webb, whitesmith
Solomon Webb
Pelatiah Webster's wife
Elijah Weed, and daughter
Edward Weir, book-binder
Charles Weifs
George Weifs, tailor
Lewis Weifs's son
John Weifman, blacksmith
J. Weifman, chocolate-maker
Philip Weifman, ditto
Catharine Weifman
John Wells, and wife
Henry Welch's child
James Welch, servant
John Welch's child
Mary Welsh
Michael Welsh, labourer, Ir.

Miles Welſh's daughter
Peter Welſh
Richard Welſh
Samuel Welſh
Thomas Welſh, tailor, wife and child
Thomas Welſh
George Weſt, houſe-carpenter
John Weſt, chair-maker
John Weſt, apprentice
Lydia Weſt
Margaret Weſt
William Weſt, bookbinder
William Weſt's wife and ſon
Henry Weſtler, hair-dreſſer, and two children
Adam Wetherſtein, butcher
John Wetherſtein, ſkin-dreſſer
George Weybel, baker, and wife
George Weyman and child
Aaron Wharton, tallowchandler
John Wharton
Mary Wharton
Peregrine Wharton, h.carpenter
Nathan Wheeler and wife
Elizabeth Wheil
Robert Wily
Edward White, labourer
Hugh White
Jacob White, apprentice
James White
James White's wife
John White
Maria White
Martha White
Matthew White
Solomon White's daughter
Charles Whitebread's child
James Whitehall's wife Mary
Joſeph Whitehead, clerk, and child, Eng.
Daniel Whitely's child
Caſpar Whiteman
Catharine Whiteman
Jane Whiteoak, Æt. 65
Hannah Whiteſides
Wm. Whiteſides, tea-merchant
John Whitman
Laurence Whitman's child
George Wibble, baker, and wife
Jacob Wickers, ferryman
Abigail Wickham's child

Jeremiah Wieſer, drayman
Michael Widner, tailor
George Wier
John Wigden, ſchool-maſter, wife and child
Samuel Wigford, hatter
Ann Wight
William Wild
Abel Wiley's wife
John Wiley, ſhoemaker, & ſiſter
Ann Wiley
John Wilkins
Mary Wilkins
James Wilkinſon, Ir.
Roderick Wilkinſon
Catharine Will, ſervant
Charles Williams, grazier
Elizabeth Williams
James Williams, tailor
John Williams and wife
John Williams's child
John Williams, coachman
Mary, widow of Joſ. Williams
Thomas Williams, mariner
Widow Williams
Jeremiah Williamſon, ſailor
Margaret Williamſon
Violet Williamſon
Mary Willing
Hugh Wills
Ann Wilſon
Charles Wilſon, clerk
Elizabeth Wilſon
James Wilſon, ferryman
James Wilſon
Jenny Wilſon
John Wilſon, h. carpenter
John Wilſon, ſailor
John Wilſon, wheelwright
John Wilſon, bricklayer
Capt. John Wilſon
Joſeph Wilſon's child
M'Calla Wilſon
Mrs. Wilſon, ſchool-miſtreſs
Richard Wilſon, ſhoemaker
Roderic Wilſon, ſailor
Wife of Wm. Wilſon, ſtationer
William Wilſon's child
William Wilſon, ſailor
Dorothy Wiltberger
Wife and child of Alexander Windſey, ſailor

Rev. John Winkhaufe & child
JohnLudwig Winkler, labourer
Mary Winkler
—— Winne, coachmaker
Child of Jac. Winnemore, grocer
Frederick Winter, failor
Wife of Jacob Winter, fhip-
carpenter
Margaret Winter
Alexander Winthrop's wife
Daniel Wife, tailor
Hannah, wife of Thos. Wife
Widow Wifeman
Benjamin Wiftar
John Witman
Peter Wittefs's fon
Chriftopher Woelpert's daugh-
ter
Elizabeth Wolf, widow
Mary Wolf
Elizabeth Wollard, fervant
Andrew Wood, currier
Catharine Wood
Cornelius Wood's wife
Elizabeth Wood
Francis Wood's child
G. Wood's daughter Rebecca
John Wood, watch-maker
John Wood, coach-man
Jona. Wood, carter, and wife
Ifaac Wood's child
Leighton Wood's wife
Mary Wood
Thomas Wood, fhoemaker
William Wood
Wafhington, fon of William
Woodhoufe, printer
Jofeph Woodman
Margaret Woodward
Chriftian Wool, tailor
James Worftall, ftore-keeper
Hannah Wrap
Jacob Wright, chairmaker
Jane Wright
Jofeph Wright, painter, and
wife
Mary Ann Wright
Sufannah Wright

Richard Wright's daughter
Catharine Wrightner
Sarah Wrinkle
Henry Wuiftler, hair-dreffer,
and child
Widow Wurftler and child
Widow Wyand's child
Child of Wm. Wyat, labourer
George Wyner, fhoemaker,
and two children
Thomas Wyner
William Wynn
John Yates, fervant
Mary Yates, widow
Catharine Yeiger
Margaret Yeoman
George Yopes, apprentice
Michael Yopes, ditto
Nelly Yorks
Phœbe York
John Youch, grocer
Catharine Young
Elizabeth Young
George Young's daughter
Jacob Young's fon
Daughter and fon-in-law of Ja-
cob Young, tailor
Jacob Young, fhoemaker
James Young and apprentice
Margaret Young
Mary Young
Michael Young and wife
Nich. Young, labourer, & wife
Plumber Young
Agnes, wife of William Young,
printer
William Young, apprentice
Chriftopher Youft's wife
Rebecca Youft
Andrew Yfenhood's 2 children
Jane Zagey
Wm. Zane's wife
Mary Zentler
John George Zeyfinger, prin-
ter
Wm. Zill
Tobias Zink's wife
Philip Zwoller

C O N T E N T S.

CPSIA information can be obtained
at www.ICGtesting.com
Printed in the USA
BVHW040902160119
537965BV00009B/169/P